100 YEARS OF

NOTRE DAME

FOOTBALL TRIVIA

THOMAS G. JOSEPH
RICHARD H. WALWOOD

QUINLAN PRESS
BOSTON

Published by Quinlan Press
131 Beverly Street
Boston, MA 02114

Cover design by Richard H. Walwood
Cover photo by Vince Wehby, Jr.

Library of Congress
Catalog Card Number 87-61321
ISBN 1-55770-000-1

Printed in the United States of America
October 1987

To my father George, my mother Helen and my brother Jim, whose spirit and encouragement during my student years established our membership in the Notre Dame family, and to my wife Janice and my five wonderful children Susan, Richard, Peter, Janice and Julie, whose love and patience are as much a part of this book as the words and photos.

R.H.W.

God has blessed me in many ways. I was privileged to have had a father whose name I share and who left this world much too young, but handed down a legacy of sportsmanship, fair play and good example.

My darkest days have been brightened by the love of a wonderful and talented wife and three lovely daughters. All of them deserve recognition for their influence, encouragement and patience.

Most of all, however, and with the deepest of everlasting gratitude, I want to thank my mother, Mae, whose sense of devotion, dedication and persistence was solely responsible for my attending such a wondrous place as the University of Notre Dame.

T.G.J.

Thomas G. Joseph is a 1959 graduate of the University of Notre Dame and a vice president of the Olympic International Bank and Trust Company in Boston. He has maintained his ties with his alma mater through involvement with the Alumni Association, as a director, as treasurer of the Notre Dame Club of Boston and as a member of the Sorin Society of Notre Dame. He lives in Milton, Massachusetts, with his wife Elizabeth and their three children, Maria, Theresa and Eileen.

Richard H. Walwood is a 1960 graduate of the University of Notre Dame. He has practiced architecture since 1966 in his own architectural firm in Milton, Massachusetts. He has maintained alumni activity through the Notre Dame Club of Boston as a director and past president. He resides in Milton, Massachusetts, with his wife, Janice Kickham Walwood, and their five children, Susan, Richard, Peter, Janice and Julie.

We wish to thank the following individuals for their assistance and cooperation:

- Dan Reagan, executive director of the Edward Frederick Sorin Society of the University of Notre Dame, for his invaluable help in directing us to the right sources for our research;

- Jethro Kyles, curator of Notre Dame's International Sports and Games Research Library for providing us with the tools to verify our facts;

- The staff of the archives at the University of Notre Dame, with a particular thanks to Sharon Sumpter, archives associate, and Charles Lamb, graphics curator, with whom we viewed the beginnings of this extraordinary football tradition;

- Associate Sports Information Director John Heisler and his secretary, Pam Holmes, for their kindness and generosity with press releases and photographs;

- Mary Ellen McKenna, our own shining star, for spending countless hours deciphering our hieroglyphics. She is indeed one of the Fighting Irish, "strong of heart and true to her name"!

The first report of Notre Dame varsity football appeared in Notre Dame Scholastic *on November 26, 1887, in a column entitled "Local Items":*

"Captain Duffy of the Ann Arbor team seemed to think we have material for an excellent football team."

Captain Duffy had no idea how prophetic his statement was.

Contents

The format of this book is intended to give the reader an experience as exhilarating as a visit to the Notre Dame campus on a fall football weekend in any of the past one hundred years. Our historic trivia sketch should take you on the same wave of excitement that players, students, alumni and subway alumni have journeyed. College football as it is played and enjoyed by the Notre Dame family is the most public manifestation of what is commonly known as the "Spirit of Notre Dame." On five or six weekends each fall this spirit is exhibited in the frenzied enthusiasm of Friday night's Pep Rally. By Saturday morning the campus population grows sevenfold with alumni and fans from all corners of America. Game time brings the entire campus to the stadium where all await the Fighting Irish exit from the tunnel. At the moment the team emerges on the field the band plays "The Notre Dame Victory March."

You are now in the stadium and will experience our game plan from loosening up, the initial contact, the momentum swings as the game wears on and the going gets tougher, and ultimately the thrill of yet another Notre Dame victory.

The opposing teams are lined up, tension mounts, the band plays, fans rise in the stands, the referee's whistle blows and it is time for . . .

KICKOFF
Cheer, cheer for Old Notre Dame . . .

1. Who was ND's first football opponent?

2. Where did ND play its home games before the construction of the present stadium?

3. Who scored ND's first touchdown?

4. Who was the university president when inter-collegiate football began at ND?

5. What was ND's first football win?

6. In what year was "The Notre Dame Victory March" introduced?

7. When was the first game away from home?

8. What former ND player has a professional football stadium named in his honor?

9. Who was ND's only player, captain and coach in the same season?

10. The mosaic on the ND library is fondly known as "Touchdown Jesus." What similar names do three campus statues have?

11. What is the official name of ND's football stadium?

12. How many times has the Associated Press selected the Fighting Irish among the top twenty?

13. What made George Gipp's attendance at Notre Dame unusual?

University of Notre Dame Archives

14. Captain Duffy of the Ann Arbor team was well acquainted with these ND athletes. Who are they?

15. George Gipp first made national sports headlines as a freshman in 1916. Why?

16. What was Knute Rockne's longest unbeaten streak?

17. What was Gipp's fatal illness?

18. Where and when was Knute Rockne born?

19. What were the circumstances of Rockne's death?

20. When, where and against whom did the famous Dorais-Rockne forward passing game take place?

21. What innovation did Rockne develop that sent college football into an uproar?

22. Where is Knute Rockne's home town?

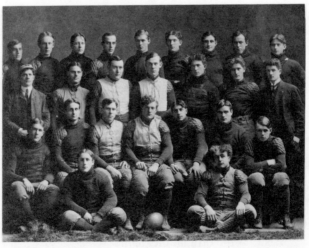

University of Notre Dame Archives

23. This ND team of 1903 holds a record that can never be surpassed. What is it?

24. How old was George Gipp at the time of his death?

25. Did Knute Rockne ever play pro football?

26. How many game, season or career team records are still held by George Gipp?

27. How large was the student enrollment at ND in George Gipp's last year?

28. Where was George Gipp born?

29. What was ND's record during George Gipp's career?

30. Who were Rockne's "Shock Troops"?

31. When was the first homecoming game played at ND?

32. Where was Knute Rockne's office?

33. Knute Rockne introduced many modifications in football. What prompted his suggestion to have opposing teams wear uniforms of contrasting color?

34. What team has the most victories over ND?

35. What famous football coach never defeated a Notre Dame team?

36. When did the University adopt "The Fighting Irish" as the official nickname?

University of Notre Dame Archives

37. This rare photograph marks the turning point in ND football history. Why?

38. Who succeeded Knute Rockne as head coach?

39. Who caught the winning pass in the famous 18–13 comeback victory over Ohio State in 1935?

40. Who holds ND's career punting average record?

41. What ND football player was elected captain but died before he ever assumed the responsibility?

42. What did Ara Parseghian, Knute Rockne and George Gipp have in common?

43. Name the "Original Four Horsemen" from the Book of Apocalypse as recorded by St. John.

44. Name the two major college football teams that do not "redshirt."

45. Name the birthplace of Frank Leahy.

46. What is ND's longest unbeaten streak?

47. Who was the "Springfield Rifle"?

48. This great ND quarterback was named to 18 First-Team All-American teams in two years. Who was he?

University of Notre Dame Archives

49. The 1913 team had nine starters other than the passing combination of Dorais and Rockne. Can you name them?

50. What is the worst defeat in ND history?

51. ND has had six Heisman Trophy winners, more than any other school. Who are they?

52. Who was the first quarterback to lead an ND team in passing yardage?

53. What two-time All-American end won the Rockne Trophy as the outstanding college lineman of the year in 1942?

54. What was Frank Leahy's record in 1941, his first season as head coach?

55. Name the 1945 Second-Team All-American and Irish captain immediately preceding Johnny Lujack as quarterback.

56. Most fans are familiar with the famous 0–0 tie with Army in 1946, but few remember that another Leahy team locked up with Army in another 0–0 tie. In what year did that game take place?

57. When did ND play West Point for the first time in South Bend?

University of Notre Dame Archives

58. Name this player, ND's first First-Team All-American.

7

59. Where was the coaching office during the Frank Leahy era?

60. How many ND quarterbacks have passed for over 2,000 yards in a season?

61. What is ND's bowl record?

62. What famous pro Hall-of-Fame coach played for "Horseman" Jim Crowley during his college career?

63. How many bowls has ND played in?

64. Who succeeded Joe Kuharich as coach?

65. What great Heisman-Trophy-winning quarterback became a professional football Hall-of-Fame running back?

66. What was ND's worst defeat at home?

67. Who scored the winning touchdown that ended Oklahoma's 47-game winning streak in 1957?

68. In what year did players wear numbers on their helmets?

69. In the 1954 USC game, ND was behind, 17–14, with 5:57 left when Ralph Guglielmi pitched out to his halfback, who sped 72 yards for the winning score. Name him.

70. What are the official colors of ND?

71. Through 1986, what team has more career victories than ND in college football history?

72. ND has had three "consensus" All-American linebackers. Who are they?

73. Which team has played ND most often in a bowl game?

University of Notre Dame Archives

74. What was this distinguished scholar-athlete's four-year grade point average at ND?

75. What ND running back and captain was badly wounded in Viet Nam and came back to star for the Pittsburgh Steelers?

76. What pro team did Ara Parseghian play for?

77. What football captain in the "Era of Ara" had the same name as a famous Civil War general?

78. What distinction does Heisman Trophy winner John Huarte hold in Heisman history?

79. What was the result of ND's first bowl appearance since 1925?

80. In 1913, the Dorais-Rockne passing combo practiced through the summer perfecting their passing game. What other famous passing combo did the same in one California summer in the sixties?

81. ND split with tradition by picking a nonalumnus when Ara Parseghian took over the coaching reins. Where did Parseghian graduate from?

82. Who was the first black ND quarterback?

83. Ara Parseghian lost only 17 games in his 11-year coaching tenure at ND. Eleven of those 17 losses were against which two teams?

84. ND has had two pass receivers in history gain over 1,000 yards. Who are they?

85. What sophomore passing combination led ND to a national championship in 1966?

86. Who was the captain of Ara Parseghian's 1966 national champions?

87. Who broke Terry Hanratty's all-time total offense record?

University of Notre Dame Archives

88. How many field goals did George Gipp kick in his varsity career?

89. Who was the opposing quarterback in Ara Parseghian's first home game at ND?

90. Which team defeated ND three years in a row during the Parseghian era?

91. What postgame tradition did Ara Parseghian establish?

92. Who holds the Irish record for kicking the most consecutive extra points?

93. What was Ara Parseghian's coaching record at ND?

94. Who holds the Irish record for most number of punts returned in a season?

95. Who was captain of Ara Parseghian's first football team in 1964?

96. What is Ara Parseghian's middle name?

97. Where was the world premier of *Knute Rockne All-American* held?

98. Where is Clashmore Mike, the second in a series of Irish Terrier ND mascots buried?

99. How many Notre Dame coaches had undefeated, untied seasons?

100. How many of the 56 Heisman Trophy winners have played against ND?

University of Notre Dame Archives

101. What characterized the Rockne style of football?

102. This 1984 AP All-American tight end has gone on to Super Bowl and All-Pro honors. Name him.

103. What former Notre Dame quarterback is the leading lifetime passer in pro football?

104. Who holds the ND career interception record?

105. Who holds the team record for most touchdowns scored in a season?

106. He gained 303 yards in 23 carries against the Irish in 1975, the most ever against an ND team. Name him.

107. Which ND head coach was the only one to have more than one losing season?

108. Tim Brown returned 25 kickoffs for 698 yards for ND in 1986. Whose school record did he surpass?

109. Brown also broke a 23-year record when he averaged 2.3 kickoff returns per game (25 returns in 11 games) for the 1986 season. Name the sixties Irish back whose record was toppled.

110. How large was university enrollment in the year of Dan Devine's national champions?

111. Who holds the ND record for most punts in a career?

112. Can you name the All-American defensive end who recovered an Alabama fumble at the Alabama four to set up ND's 7–0 win over the Crimson Tide in 1980?

113. What distinction did Notre Dame earn with this win?

KICKOFF — ANSWERS

1. The University of Michigan, which beat ND, 8–0, on November 23, 1887

2. Cartier Field

3. Harry Jewett, on a five-yard run against Michigan on April 20, 1888

4. Rev. Thomas Walsh, C.S.C., president, 1881–1893

5. ND beat the Harvard School of Chicago, 20–0, on December 6, 1888.

6. February 22, 1909, during a Washington's Birthday celebration — it was played for the first time at an athletic event approximately ten years later.

7. On November 14, 1889, at Northwestern

8. Lambeau Field, Green Bay, Wisconsin, was named after Earl (Curley) Lambeau.

9. Frank E. Hering, 1896

10. "Faircatch" Corby, "Dropkick" Jesus and "We're Number 1" Moses

11. Notre Dame Stadium

12. Thirty-five times in 51 years

13. He was the son of devout Protestant parents.

14. The 1887 ND squad: Frank Fehr, LE; Patrick Nelson, LT; Edward Sawkins, LG; George Houck, C; Frank Springer, RG; Tom O'Regan, RT; James Maloney, RE; George Cartier, QB; Joe Cusack, LH; Henry Luhn (captain), RH; and Harry Jewett, FB

15. On November 11, 1916, while playing on the freshman squad against Western State Normal (now Western Michigan), Gipp dropkicked a 62-yard field goal for a 10–7 ND victory. At the time it was thought to be the longest field goal in football history.

16. Twenty-two games (1918–1921)

17. He contracted a strep throat after the Northwestern game and died from complications of the disease on December 14, 1920.

18. Voss, Norway, on March 4, 1888

19. He was killed in a plane crash near Bazaar, Kansas, on March 31, 1931.

20. In 1913 at West Point against Army

21. The ND shift

22. Chicago, Illinois

23. They were unscored upon in a nine-game season. Featured on the team were Louis "Red" Salmon (front row, center), ND's first All-American, and Henry J. "Fuzzy" McGlew (lower right), later head coach in 1905.

24. Twenty-five

25. Only briefly, with the Massillon, Ohio, Tigers

26. Four — rushing yards per attempt in a season: 8.1 (102/827), in 1920; total kickoff returns in a game: eight (157 yards) in 1920; total offensive yards per attempt in a season: 9.37 (164/1536) in 1920; total kick returns in a game: ten (2PR, 8KR/207) in 1920.

27. 1,207 students

28. Laurium, Michigan, on February 18, 1895

29. 27–2–3 (1917 to 1920)

30. Substitutes who played the first four or five minutes of the first and third quarters. This led to the two platoon system.

31. On November 6, 1920, ND beat Purdue, 28–0.

32. On the second floor, rear center, of the administration building

33. A 1921 loss to Iowa caused by an interception

34. Southern California with 23 victories

35. Paul "Bear" Bryant (0–4–0)

36. In 1927, during the tenure of Fr. Matthew Walsh, C.S.C.

37. It shows Knute Rockne catching a touchdown pass from Gus Dorais in ND's historic win over Army in 1913.

38. "Hunk" Anderson

39. Wayne Millner

40. Bill Shakespeare (40.71)

41. Joe Sullivan, 1935, who died from complications of pneumonia in March 1935

42. All were Protestants; Rockne later converted to Catholicism, and Gipp's "conversion" has been the subject of controversy.

43. Famine, Pestilence, Destruction and Death

44. ND and Duke University

45. Winner, South Dakota

46. Thirty-nine (two ties) (1946–50) under head coach Frank Leahy

47. Angelo Bertelli

48. Johnny Lujack, 1946–47

49. Deak Jones, LT; Emmett Keefe, LG; Al Feeney, C; Freeman Fitzgerald, RG; Zipper Lathrop, RT; Fred Gushurst, RE; Charles Finegan, LH; Joe Pliska, RH; and Ray Eichenlaub, FB

50. Army beat ND, 59–0, in 1944.

51. Angelo Bertelli, quarterback, 1943; Johnny Lujack, quarterback, 1947; Leon Hart, end, 1949; Johnny Lattner, halfback, 1953; Paul Hornung, quarterback, 1956; and John Huarte, quarterback, 1964

52. Angelo Bertelli in 1941, ND's first T-formation quarterback

53. Bob Dove

54. 8–0–1

55. Frank "Boley" Dancewicz (1943–1945)

56. 1941

57. 1947, in their 33d encounter

58. Quarterback Gus Dorais (1913)

59. Breen Phillips Hall

60. Four: John Huarte, 1964; Joe Theismann, 1970; Joe Montana, 1978; and Steve Beuerlein, 1986

61. 8–4–0

62. Vince Lombardi, one of Fordham's "Seven Blocks of Granite"

63. Seven: Rose, Cotton, Orange, Sugar, Gator, Aloha and Liberty

64. Hugh Devore in 1963

65. Paul Hornung, Green Bay Packers

66. Oklahoma beat ND in 1956, 40–0.

67. Dick Lynch

68. 1958 under Terry Brennan

69. Jim Morse

70. Gold and Blue

71. The University of Michigan, 676 — ND is second with 651.

72. Bob Crable, 1980 and 1981; Bob Golic, 1978; and Jim Lynch, 1966

73. Texas has played ND three times, in 1970, 1971 and 1978, in the Cotton Bowl.

74. Knute Rockne achieved a 90.52 average (on a score of a hundred) and graduated magnum cum laude in chemistry.

75. Rocky Bleier

76. The Cleveland Browns

77. Phil Sheridan, 1965

78. He is the only returning nonletterman to win the award.

79. ND lost to Texas, 21–17, in the Cotton Bowl on January 1, 1970.

80. John Huarte and Jack Snow in the summer of 1964 — Huarte was rebuilding a separated shoulder.

81. Miami of Ohio

82. Cliff Brown, 1971

83. USC (6) and Purdue (5)

84. Jack Snow, 1964 (1,114 yards) and Tom Gatewood, 1970 (1,123 yards)

85. Terry Hanratty and Jim Seymour

86. Jim Lynch

87. Joe Theismann against Pitt in 1970

88. Despite his powerful kicking ability, Gipp kicked only one field goal in his varsity career, against Indiana in 1919.

89. Bob Griese, Purdue

90. Purdue in 1967, 1968 and 1969

91. Presentation of the game ball to a senior for career contributions

92. Bob Thomas, 62 (from November 6, 1971 to October 20, 1973)

93. 95–17–4, .836

94. Tom Schoen with 42 punt returns in 1967

95. Jim Carroll

96. Raoul

97. In the Palace and the Granada Theatres, South Bend, Indiana, on October 4, 1940

98. Under the turf in the ND stadium

99. Five: John L. Marks in 1912; Jesse Harper in 1913; Knute Rockne in 1919, 1920, 1924, 1929 and 1930; Frank Leahy in 1947 and 1949; and Ara Parseghian in 1973

100. Nineteen

101. Rockne believed in speed and deception as opposed to size and strength. By utilizing the movement and momentum of the "Notre Dame Shift," his smaller, swifter players had the ability to score from any part of the field. This often resulted in what Rockne termed "the perfect play."

102. Mark Bavaro, of the New York Giants

103. Joe Montana, of the San Francisco 49ers (career rating 92.4)

104. Luther Bradley, with 17 interceptions in 1973, 1975, 1976 and 1977

105. Allen Pinkett, with 18 touchdowns scored in both 1983 and 1984

106. Tony Dorsett, the University of Pittsburgh

107. Gerry Faust, 1981 and 1985 — he was 5-6-0 both seasons.

108. Jim Stone, 19 returns for 493 yards in 1979

109. Bill Wolski, 1.8 returns per game

110. 8,750 students

111. Blair Kiel, with 259 punts from 1980 to 1983

112. Scott Zettek

113. The Irish win was the first shutout of Alabama on its home field in 22 years.

FIRST QUARTER
. . . wake up the echoes cheering her name . . .

1. Who was ND's first football captain?

2. Name the only team to play ND twice in one season.

3. Who was ND's first two-time football captain?

4. Against what team did ND score its most one-sided victory?

5. Who is the only undefeated coach in Irish history?

6. What was the record of the 1913 team that Knute Rockne captained?

7. Who was ND's first head football coach?

8. Where on the ND campus was the first football game played?

9. Who coached the fewest number of games at ND?

10. What is the Blue-Gold game?

11. What is the longest continuous intersectional rivalry in college football history?

12. What is the record crowd-size for a Blue-Gold game?

13. Why was the sod relocated from Cartier Field to the new stadium in 1929?

University of Notre Dame Archives

14. Name these members of the Miller clan of Defiance, Ohio, who distinguished themselves as one of ND's first families.

15. Why was ND's football team known as the "Ramblers"?

16. What was the name of Knute Rockne's wife?

17. Which ND player was the only leading rusher, passer and scorer three years in a row?

18. What was the worst defeat suffered under Knute Rockne?

19. Who are ND's subway alumni?

20. Who was the first ND player selected on Walter Camp's First String All-American team?

21. Who coached the most number of games at ND?

22. What request did a dying George Gipp allegedly make to Knute Rockne?

23. How many ND players and coaches have been elected to the National Football Foundation Hall of Fame?

Boston Public Library, Print Department

24. Each member of this Irish backfield earned All-America status. Who are they?

25. This 1921 All-American end made the National Football Foundation Hall of Fame as a coach. Who was he?

26. Two other former players made it the same way. Name them.

27. Who holds the ND season record for highest average yards per carry (100 attempts minimum)?

28. The 1921 season was recognized as the first of Knute Rockne's "suicide seasons." Why?

29. Who succeeded George Gipp as offensive leader at ND?

30. What was Knute Rockne's middle name?

31. Who holds the record for single-game all-purpose yards (rushing, receiving and returns)?

32. Who captained the 1920 national championship team?

33. Name the singularly most adversarial media personality to Knute Rockne.

34. What was the "Taylorville Game"?

35. Who was the first ND end to be chosen All-American?

36. Only two teams have defeated ND more than 20 times. Name them.

37. What precedent was established when ND played Stanford in the 1925 Rose Bowl?

38. What team has the most NCAA consensus All-Americans?

39. ND has had seven consensus All-American centers, two of which came from the same hometown. Who were they and what was their hometown?

40. Who was ND's first two-sport All-American?

Boston Public Library, Print Department

41. Name these early 1930s players who had famous relatives precede them as team members.

42. What All-American guard became sergeant-at-arms for the U.S. Senate?

43. How large was the ND student enrollment at the beginning of the Leahy years?

44. Who was the All-American lineman who centered five perfect snaps to Marchy Schwartz in ND's end zone despite one hand in a cast and the other deeply gashed?

45. Who are the two winningest coaches (percentage) in college football history?

46. One of collegiate football's greatest intersectional rivalries is the series between ND and the University of Southern California. When did this series begin?

47. ND has had 67 consensus All-Americans in its history. Only two fullbacks have achieved this honor. Who are they?

48. How many Ivy League opponents have played against ND?

49. Who coached ND in 1944 and 1945 due to Frank Leahy's service absence?

50. Known for his humor, wit and personality, this 230-pound tackle could also play football and was voted to two First-Team All-American Squads in 1947. Name him.

51. What NBA all-star player's father was an ND quarterback?

52. What was Frank Leahy's coaching record at ND?

53. This great quarterback won the Heisman Trophy despite the fact that he did not lead his team in passing that season. Name him.

54. What ND coach had the most undefeated seasons?

55. What ND captain was named All-American at two schools?

56. Who had the longest run from scrimmage without scoring?

57. In 1944 where did the Irish rank in the AP poll despite imposing defeats to Army and Navy?

58. Only one opposing team defeated a Frank Leahy coached team more than once; name the team.

59. What Second-Team All-American sophomore halfback left ND after two years to enter the Naval Academy?

60. Who was captain of Frank Leahy's first ND team in 1941?

61. Of all the famous ND running backs, who was the only one to win an NCAA rushing title?

62. Name the ten opponents ND has played most frequently.

63. Name the men above who carried on where "Rock" left off at ND in the 1931 season.

64. Who was ND's first All-American defensive back?

65. Since the AP rankings started in 1936, how many times has ND been voted among the top ten teams in the nation?

66. How many ND coaches came up from the ranks of assistant coaches?

67. How large was the ND student enrollment at the end of the Leahy era?

68. ND had one head coach who served at two different periods. Who was he?

69. What was ND's record the year Paul Hornung won the Heisman Trophy?

70. Only one ND head coach also led ND in scoring as a player. Name him.

71. In what year did ND players wear shamrocks on their helmets and UCLA-style shoulder stripes on their jerseys?

Boston Public Library, Print Department

72. Name this "Irish" backfield of 1932.

73. What is the largest crowd ever to witness a game at Notre Dame Stadium?

74. When was the last time ND played an Ivy League opponent?

75. What ND player holds the record for most touchdown passes in a game?

76. What is the longest losing streak to a single opponent in ND history?

77. What ND player was drafted and signed by the New York Jets the same year as Joe Namath?

78. Where did pep rallies take place after the fieldhouse was torn down?

79. Who were known as "Fling and Cling"?

80. How did Nick Eddy injure himself prior to the 1966 Michigan State 10–10 tie?

81. What Michigan State student cheer followed the player to the pros?

82. Following the famous 1966, 10–10 tie with Michigan State, the Irish headed west to face their old nemesis, the Rose Bowl-bound University of Southern California Trojans. What was the final score?

83. Who was the first ND player to surpass George Gipp in total offense?

84. What opposing player's photo was taped to sidewalks throughout the ND campus allowing students to "walk all over him"?

85. Who said, "You could be the first class to graduate without having a winning season"?

86. Why did Ara Parseghian change his mind about accepting the ND position of head coach?

87. This great consensus All-American still holds the ND record for most touchdown receptions in a season. Who is he?

88. This consensus All-American safety holds the ND season and career record for most career punt returns for touchdowns. Name him.

Boston Public Library, Print Department

89. Name this hero of the 1935 "Game of the Century."

90. Ara Parseghian teams were shut out only once. When?

91. In 1965 what was the inscription on a sign hung on the dome of the administration building at ND?

92. Name this 1970 consensus All-American receiver who holds Irish records for receptions and reception yardage both in a career and a season.

93. Whose career and season records did he eclipse?

94. What nickname did John Huarte's teammates bestow upon him?

95. What was the worst total offensive production in a game under Ara Parseghian?

96. This consensus All-American defensive back was NCAA leader in punt return yardage in 1965. Name him.

97. Where was the coaching office during the Ara Parseghian era?

Boston Public Library, Print Department

98. Why the happy faces?

99. How many rows are there in the Notre Dame Stadium?

100. What ND coaches previously coached teams against ND?

101. Who holds the record for most rushing attempts in a game?

102. What is the longest pass play in ND history?

103. What season was Dan Devine's least productive?

104. ND has played one game outside of the U.S.A. When did this take place?

105. Who holds the ND record for most rushing attempts in a season?

106. Name this two-time consensus All-American linebacker from the Dan Devine era.

107. Who was Dan Devine's toughest opponent?

108. Allen Pinkett broke the ND record for most 100-yard rushing games in a season. How many games and whose record did he beat?

109. Who holds the single-season ND record for most fumble recoveries?

110. On September 15, 1979, ND pulled a thrilling come-from-behind victory against Michigan, 12–10, on the toe of this powerful Irish kicker who kicked four field goals. Name him.

111. This same game was not decided until the final seven seconds, when a 42-yard Michigan field goal attempt was blocked by what ND player?

112. Name the assistant coach whose "little" brother played for him.

FIRST QUARTER — ANSWERS

1. Henry Luhn (1887)

2. The University of Michigan (April 20 and 21, 1888), which won both games, 24-6 and 10-4

3. Edward C. Prudhomme, 1888 and 1889

4. ND beat American Medical of Chicago, 142-0, in 1905.

5. John L. Marks (13-0-2 from 1911 to 1912)

6. 7-0-0

7. James L. Morison, 1894

8. On a field currently occupied by the Chemistry Building and Nieuwland Hall of Science

9. H. G. Hadden, who coached four games in 1895

10. Annual finale for spring football practice

11. Navy-Notre Dame, 1927 to present

12. 35,675 in 1981, Gerry Faust's first spring game

13. Because ND had not lost on it in 23 years.

14. Left to right: Don, Gerry, Walter, Ray and Harry ("Red") — Harry had two sons, Tom and Creighton, who continued their familiy's contribution.

15. Rockne's teams were the first in the nation to travel throughout the country battling opponents.

16. Bonnie Skiles Rockne

17. George Gipp (1918 through 1920)

18. When ND lost to Army 27–0 in 1925

19. ND fans who, although they are not actual alumni, have adopted the university as their own

20. George Gipp, 1920

21. Knute Rockne coached 122 games between 1918 and 1930.

22. "Some day when things are bad, and the breaks are going against us, ask the boys to go out and win one for me."

23. Twenty-eight players and five coaches

24. Left to right: Jim Crowley, Don Miller, Harry Stuhldreher and Elmer Layden – a.k.a. "The Four Horsemen"

25. Eddie Anderson, 1918–1921

26. Charlie Bachman, 1914–1916; and Frank Thomas, 1920–1922

27. George Gipp, 8.1 yards per carry in 1920

28. In an 11-game season, Rockne scheduled seven major opponents: Iowa, Purdue, Nebraska, Indiana, Army, Rutgers and Michigan State.

29. HB Johnny Mohardt (Second-Team Walter Camp All-American, 1921)

30. Kenneth

31. Willie Maher – 361 yards (107 rushing, 80 punt returns, 174 kick returns against Kalamazoo, 1923)

32. Frank Coughlin, left tackle

33. Westbrook Pegler

34. A semiprofessional encounter between players from ND and Illinois in 1921 which prompted Rockne to turn down a Rose Bowl bid that year on ethical grounds

35. Roger Kiley, 1920

36. Purdue (21) and USC (23)

37. It marked the first time the Irish brought its football team to the West Coast.

38. Yale University, with 69 different players. ND is second with 67.

39. Jack Robinson (1934) and John Scully (1980) – both were from Huntington, New York.

40. Moose Krause, football and basketball

41. Fred Carideo (left), cousin of Frank, and Mike Layden (right), brother of Elmer, are shown here with Coach Hunk Anderson.

42. Frank (Nordy) Hoffman, 1931

43. 3,055 students

44. Tommy Yarr, in a 0–0 tie against Northwestern in 1931

45. Knute Rockne – .881 – and Frank Leahy – .864

46. 1926

47. Emil Sitko, 1948 and 1949; and Elmer Layden, 1924

48. Four: Dartmouth, Princeton, Penn and Yale

49. Ed McKeever, 1944; Hugh Devore, 1945

50. Zygmont "Ziggy" Czarobski

51. Kelly Tripucka, son of Frank

52. 87–11–9 (.855)

53. Angelo Bertelli, who completed 25 of 36 passes, while Johnny Lujack completed 34 of 71

54. Frank Leahy had six: 1941, 1946, 1947, 1948, 1949 and 1953

55. George Connor, 1942 (Holy Cross), 1946 and 1947 (ND)

56. Emil Sitko, 83 yards against Illinois in 1946

57. Ninth

58. Michigan State, three times

59. Bob Kelly entered Annapolis in 1945.

60. Paul Lillis

61. Creighton Miller, 1943 with 911 yards

62. Navy (60), Purdue (58), USC (58), Michigan State (52), Pitt (48), Army (46), Northwestern (43), Georgia Tech (30), Indiana (28) and Iowa (24) (through 1986)

63. Left to right: Jess Harper, athletic director; Hunk Anderson, head coach; Jack Chevigny, assistant coach; and Tommy Yarr, captain

64. Tony Carey, 1964

65. Twenty-nine times in 51 years, the last time in 1980

66. Four: Hunk Anderson, Hugh Devore, Knute Rockne and Ed McKeever

67. 5,100 students

68. Hugh Devore, 1945 and 1963

69. 2–8, in 1956

70. Terry Brennan (twice), who in 1946 scored 36 points (tied with Jim Mello), and in 1947 scored 66 points

71. 1959, under Coach Joe Kuharich

72. Left to right: Joe Sheetketski, RH; Chuck Jaskwhich, QB; George Melinkovich, FB; and Mike Koken, LH

73. 61,296 against Purdue on October 6, 1962

74. 1955, when ND beat Penn, 46–14

75. Steve Beuerlein, (against USC in 1986); Daryl Lamonica (against Pitt in 1962); and Angelo Bertelli (against Stanford in 1942) — all with four

76. Two streaks of eight: Michigan — 1887, 1888 (two games), 1898, 1899, 1900, 1902 and 1908; Michi-

gan State – 1955, 1956, 1957, 1959, 1960, 1961, 1962 and 1963

77. John Huarte

78. Stepan Center

79. Terry Hanratty and Jim Seymour

80. Getting off the train in East Lansing

81. "Kill, Bubba, Kill" (for Bubba Smith, of course!)

82. ND 51, USC 0

83. Terry Hanratty in a 1967 victory over Illinois University

84. Anthony Davis, University of Southern California, prior to the 1973 game

85. Ara Parseghian, in his first team meeting in 1964

86. He questioned his right to coach ND because he was not a Catholic.

87. Jack Snow – nine in 1964

88. Nick Rassas – three between 1963 and 1965

89. Andy Pilney led the underdog Irish to an 18–13 comeback victory over Ohio State in Columbus.

90. Miami, 0–0 tie in 1965

91. "Remember" — prior to the USC game in 1965. This was a reference to the last-minute loss to USC in 1964 that cost ND a national championship.

92. Tom Gatewood (1969–1971). In his three years of varsity play, he caught 157 passes for 2,283 yards, and in 1970 alone, he had 77 receptions for 1,123 yards, both ND records.

93. Jim Seymour's in both categories

94. "Stevie Wonder"

95. Twelve total yards in the 1965 Michigan State game. The Irish lost, 12–3.

96. Nick Rassas, 459 yards in 24 carries

97. Rockne Memorial Building

98. First-year Irish coach Frank Leahy is congratulating Captain Wally Ziemba and Steve Juzwik at the end of the undefeated 1941 season, the first at ND since 1930, Rockne's last team.

99. Sixty

100. Dan Devine, 0–1–1 with Missouri; Ara Parseghian, 4–0–0 with Northwestern; and Jess Harper, 0–3–0 with Wabash

101. Allen Pinkett (40 attempts for 162 yards against LSU in 1984), and Phil Carter (40 for 254 yards against Michigan State in 1980)

102. Blair Kiel to Joe Howard, 96 yards (Georgia Tech, 1981)

103. 1979 – 7-4-0

104. 1979 – the Mirage Bowl at Tokyo, Japan. ND beat Miami, 40-15.

105. Vagas Ferguson – 301 in 1979

106. Bob Crable (1980-1981)

107. USC – he lost five times, one-third of his losses at ND.

108. Nine games in 1983. Vagas Ferguson held the previous record with seven in 1979.

109. Cedric Figaro, seven in 1986

110. Chuck Male

111. Linebacker Bob Crable

112. Mike Stock coached his brother Jim Stock.

SECOND QUARTER
. . . send a volley cheer on high . . .

1. In the history of ND football, what game is considered initially most significant?

2. Who was the first ND football player to receive All-American recognition?

3. Who was the ND all-time leading career scorer prior to Allen Pinkett?

4. This future assistant Irish coach and eminent ND sports historian produced the longest punt return resulting in a touchdown. Name him.

5. Who was ND's only three-time captain?

6. When did ND win its one hundredth victory?

7. Who coached ND's only unscored upon team?

8. How large was the student enrollment at ND when its football team still had no coach (1887 to 1893)?

9. Who kicked ND's first field goal?

10. Who was ND's first full-time football coach?

11. What campus building complex occupies the site of the original Cartier Field?

University of Notre Dame, Sports Information Department

12. This ND Heisman Trophy winner won the award despite playing in only six of ten games.

13. How many teams hold a career winning record (six games or more) over ND?

14. What state has produced the most ND consensus All-Americans?

15. When was the "Block" ND logo first used?

16. Name the members of the "Four Horsemen" back-field (1922–1924).

17. Can you recall the words that forever immortal-ized these four backfield stars?

18. Who labeled them the "Four Horsemen"?

19. The largest attendance for a season during Rockne's coaching tenure was 551,112 in a nine-game season in 1929. When was this record surpassed?

20. Who was the first collegiate sports information director of ND?

21. What was ND's first bowl game?

22. Who was the coach of ND's first bowl opponent?

23. What were George Gipp's statistics in one of the greatest player performances in collegiate football history against Army in 1920?

24. What were George Gipp's plans after college?

University of Notre Dame, Sports Information Department

25. For what famous movie role was this player screen-tested?

26. When was George Gipp's last game?

27. Who holds the ND record for most kickoff return yards in a single game?

28. Harry Stuhldreher, the quarterback in the ND "Four Horsemen" backfield, hails from what fabled football town?

29. During the era 1922–1924, the "Four Horsemen" lost only two games, both to the same team. Name the team.

30. Who were the "Seven Mules"?

31. Prior to the first 2,000-yard passer, what player held the ND record for total offense (rushing and passing) in a season?

32. In 1923 Don Miller scored ten touchdowns to share the Irish scoring title with what other running back?

33. Who was the 165-pound center of the early 1920s who gained Walter Camp's Second Team All-American by battling opposing linemen outweighing him by 65 to 70 pounds?

34. What famous sportswriter covered South Bend sports including ND football during George Gipp's playing days?

35. What was the average weight of the "Seven Mules," the ND linemen of 1924?

36. Where does legend tell us George Gipp's "ghost" resides?

37. Seven ND players have led their teams in rushing, passing and scoring in one year. Name them.

38. How many times has ND been chosen as national champions by rating systems?

39. What season produced ND's least potent scoring offense?

40. What All-American replaced the injured Frank Leahy as starting right tackle?

41. Who holds the record for most punts in one game?

42. Who is the only elected captain of an ND team to resign?

43. Notre Dame Stadium was designed by the same firm as another famous American house of sport. What was it?

44. Who played Father Callahan, the fictitious university president, in the movie, *Knute Rockne, All-American*?

University of Notre Dame, Sports Information Department

45. Who is this quarterback, who lost only one game in his ND career?

46. How many losing seasons has ND had in the span of 100 years? When were they?

47. What three famous collegiate football coaches appeared in the movie, *Knute Rockne, All-American*?

48. What three-time All-American played a key role in the 1942 upset victory of Holy Cross over Boston College, 55–12?

49. What future ND All-American running back almost single-handedly defeated ND while playing for another team?

50. What was ND's longest winning streak?

51. This three-time All-American end has been voted in many polls as the greatest end in ND history. Name him.

52. Who made the game-saving open field tackle of Doc Blanchard in the 1946 ND-Army 0-0 tie?

53. Rated by many as the greatest guard in ND history, he was a consensus All-American in 1947 and 1948. Who was he?

54. What Irish Heisman Trophy winner turned down an appointment to West Point at his high school graduation ceremony?

55. What is the highest national rank in pass defense achieved by an ND team?

56. One ND team had three quarterbacks go on to pro ball. Who were the players and in what year?

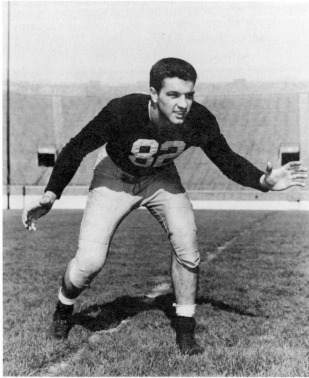

University of Notre Dame, Sports Information Department

57. This teenager distinguished himself playing with and against the cream of the World War II veterans. Name him.

58. ND has had consensus All-Americans in 47 seasons. In what season did they produce five selections?

59. In his second year of collegiate competition, this left tackle won almost unanimous recognition on

the first team All-American squad in 1943. Name him.

60. In what year did ND field only five returning lettermen?

61. This All-American end once won the National AAU indoor shot-put title with a toss of 50 feet, 2½ inches. Who was he?

62. What annual trophy goes to the winner of the ND-Purdue game?

63. How many teams hold a career winning record over ND?

64. This former assistant coach under Terry Brennan became a successful professional and Super Bowl-winning coach. Name him.

65. This ND guard was the only consensus All-American lineman on a Terry Brennan coached team. Name him.

66. Who kicked the winning field goal with 2:15 remaining to beat Iowa, 17-14, in 1955?

67. What ND halfback holds the National record for pass reception yards per catch in one game?

68. What self-imposed university rule in the fifties influenced the ND football program?

69. In 1955, when the Irish captain, Ray Lemek, was shifted from left guard to right tackle, who

replaced him at his original slot and earned AP first team All-American honors?

70. Is the ND bench on the north, south, east or west side of the field?

71. Which university president's administration saw the most head coaches?

72. Name them.

73. Name a former ND player who is the son of a Pro Football Hall of Fame enshrinee.

74. What annual trophy goes to the winner of the ND-Michigan State game?

Boston Public Library, Print Department

75. Name these four Heisman Trophy candidates of 1948 and 1949.

76. Who kicked the field goal to tie Michigan State, 10–10, in that memorable 1966 classic?

77. Who scored the only Irish touchdown that November afternoon?

78. The ND touchdown pass was a 34-yarder by a replacement quarterback who required two insulin shots a day to control his diabetes. Name him.

79. Whom did he replace?

80. The starting quarterback's injury was caused by a hard tackle by Michigan State's Charley Thornhill and another Spartan who was to achieve not only All-Pro status but a successful film career. Name him.

81. Who caught the winning pass for Southern California that prevented the 1964 Irish from a perfect season?

82. Who holds the record for most pass attempts in a game?

83. What inscription was posted over the ND Stadium's locker room exit during the Ara Parseghian era?

84. Before 1964, how much playing time had John Huarte experienced?

85. In what season was freshman eligibility reinstated?

86. Who holds the record for most pass receptions in a game?

87. What Bowl game did ND players vote to turn down?

88. What defensive alignment is commonly known as the "ND defense"?

89. What other team traditions did Ara Parseghian initiate?

90. In 1964, in Parseghian's first game as coach, how did he reward one of his "out-of-position" players?

University of Notre Dame, Sports Information Department

91. This ND back personified the meaning of triple threat. Who is he?

92. How many times did a team coached by Ara Parseghian suffer consecutive losses?

93. Who was the first starting freshman for ND after freshman eligibility was reinstated?

94. Who holds the record for the highest number of rushing yards in a game by a quarterback?

95. Of the 95 Ara Parseghian wins, how many were shutouts?

96. Who holds the ND record for most touchdown passes in a season?

97. Prior to the first 1,000-yard rusher, only five players rushed for over 800 yards in a season. Name them.

98. ND has the greatest number of academic All-Americans. How many?

99. What Irish kicker holds the school record for most consecutive field goals?

100. Who holds the Irish record for most rushing yardage gained in a game?

101. Who holds the season record for all-purpose yardage (total yardage from rushing, receiving and kick returns)?

102. Who kicked the 19-yard field goal with no time left to lift the Irish to a thrilling 38–37 victory over the University of Southern California in 1986?

103. This player's career pass-receiving records stood until the aerial shows of Hanratty to Seymour. Who is he?

104. Name the two brothers who have captained ND football teams.

105. This ND quarterback attempted 119 consecutive

passes without an interception for an Irish record. Name him.

106. What have been the most points scored in a game by an Irish team at Notre Dame Stadium?

107. What was the longest field goal ever kicked against ND?

108. What is coach Lou Holtz's alma mater?

109. Prior to coming to ND, where did he coach?

110. Name the members of this highly productive ND backfield, the last of Frank Leahy's coaching career.

111. What uniform number has appeared most often in ND's 100 years of football? What number has appeared the least?

112. What is the "Irish Guard"?

113. Who is the director/advisor of the Irish Guard?

SECOND QUARTER — ANSWERS

1.   ND's first win over Michigan in 1909, 11–3 — the Irish had lost the first eight games of the series, and this game established ND's "Western" prominence.

2.   Fullback Louis "Red" Salmon — Walter Camp Third Team honors in 1903

3.   Red Salmon scored 250 points between 1900 and 1903. Under today's scoring rules he would have totaled 282 points.

4.   Chet Grant produced the longest punt return resulting in a touchtown, 95 yards.

5.   Jack Mullen in 1887, 1888 and 1889

6.   On November 19, 1910, over Ohio Northern, 47–0, under Coach Frank "Shorty" Longman

7. James F. Faragher, 1903

8. 542 students

9. Mike Daly, against Chicago in 1897 (35 yards)

10. Frank E. Hering in 1896 (two part-time coaches, James L. Morison in 1894 and H. G. Hadden in 1895, preceded Hering)

11. Hesburgh Memorial Library Quadrangle (east of and to the rear of the O'Shaughnessy Building and Nieuwland Science Center and north of the stadium)

12. Angelo Bertelli, who was called into the Marine Corps in 1943

13. One, Michigan (5–13–0)

14. Ohio — 13 players

15. 1897 (Our research took us back to a team photo from that year, and there is no evidence that the now-famous symbol was used before that time.)

16. Elmer Layden, FB; Harry Stuhldreher, QB; Don Miller, RHB; and Jim Crowley, LHB

17. "Outlined against a blue-gray October sky, the Four Horsemen rode again. In dramatic lore they are known as Famine, Pestilence, Destruction and Death. These are only aliases. Their real names are: Stuhldreher, Miller, Crowley and Layden."

18. Grantland Rice

19. In 1947, when a Frank Leahy-coached team played before 571,527 fans in a nine-game season

20. George Strickler, a student hired by Rockne, who set up the famous Four Horsemen picture

21. The 1925 Rose Bowl against Stanford, which the Irish won, 27–10

22. Pop Warner, Stanford, 1925

23. Gipp had 480 yards of total offense (150 yards rushing, 123 yards passing and 207 yards on kick returns).

24. He had planned to join the Chicago Cubs as a center fielder.

25. George Connor for the role of Tarzan

26. November 20, 1920, against Northwestern — ND won, 22–7.

27. Paul Castner — 253 yards on four returns against Kalamazoo in 1922

28. Massillon, Ohio

29. Nebraska

30. Adam Walsh, center; Rip Miller and Joe Bach, tackles; Noble Kizer and Johnny Weibel, guards; and Ed Hunsinger and Chuck Collins, ends

31. In 1921 John Mohardt totaled 1,776 yards (781 yards rushing and 995 passing).

32. Willie "Red" Maher

33. Harvey Brown, 1923

34. Ring Lardner

35. 176 pounds

36. In Washington Hall, the university theatre where Gipp once resided

37. George Gipp (1918, 1919, 1920); John Mohardt (1921); Marchy Schwartz (1930, 1931); Nick Lukats (1933); Bill Shakespeare (1935); Bob Wilke (1936); and Paul Hornung (1956)

38. Seventeen: 1919, 1920, 1924, 1927, 1929, 1930, 1938, 1943, 1946, 1947, 1949, 1953, 1964, 1966, 1967, 1973 and 1977

39. 1933 under "Hunk" Anderson – 32 points in nine games

40. Joe Kurth

41. Marchmont "Marchy" Schwartz – 15 (for 509 yards) against Army in 1931

42. Bill Smith in 1936, due to illness

43. Yankee Stadium, which was also designed by the Osborne Engineering Company, Cleveland, Ohio

44. Donald Crisp

45. Johnny Lujack

46. Nine. They were:

Year	Record	Coach
1887	0–1–0	None
1888	0–4–0	None
1933	3–5–1	Anderson
1956	2–8–0	Brennan
1960	2–8–0	Kuharich
1963	2–7–0	Devore
1981	5–6–0	Faust
1985	5–6–0	Faust
1986	5–6–0	Holtz

47. Howard Jones (University of Southern California), Glenn (Pop) Warner (Stanford University), Amos Alonzo Stagg (Chicago)

48. George Connor

49. Emil "Six Yard" Sitko, while playing for Great Lakes Training Station in 1943. Great Lakes won, 19–14, spoiling an otherwise undefeated-untied ND season.

50. Twenty-one (1946 through 1948) under Frank Leahy

51. Leon Hart (1946–1949)

52. Johnny Lujack

53. Bill "Moose" Fischer

54. John Lujack

55. Third, in 1946

56. John Lujack, George Ratterman and Frank Tripucka in 1946

57. Leon Hart

58. 1943: Angelo Bertelli, Creighton Miller, John Yonakor, Jim White and Pat Filley

59. Jim White

60. 1944

61. John Yonakor

62. A Shillelagh

63. Seven: Chicago (4–0–0), Florida State (1–0–0), Georgia (1–0–0), Great Lakes (2–1–2), Indianapolis Artillery (1–0–0), Michigan (13–5–0) and Yale (1–0–0)

64. Hank Stram (1957–1958) who went on to coach the Kansas City Chiefs

65. Al Ecuyer, in 1957 – Ecuyer was also chosen on the UPI and Sporting News First Teams in 1958.

66. Paul Hornung

67. Jim Morse, 41.6 (5 for 208) against USC in 1955

68. A limit of 80 scholarships over four years; this was in effect for two years.

69. Pat Bisceglia

70. West

71. The administration of Rev. Theodore M. Hesburgh, C.S.C. — eight coaches between 1952 and 1986

72. Frank Leahy (1952 to 1953), Terry Brennan (1954 to 1958), Joe Kuharich (1959 to 1962), Hugh Devore (1963), Ara Parseghian (1964 to 1974), Dan Devine (1975 to 1980), Gerry Faust (1981 to 1985) and Lou Holtz (1986)

73. Bronko Nagurski, Jr.

74. A megaphone

75. Left to right: Emil "Red" Sitko (eighth in 1949), Leon Hart (first in 1949), Doak Walker of SMU (first in 1948) and Bob Williams (fifth in 1949)

76. Joe Azzaro

77. Bob Gladieux

78. Coley O'Brien

79. Terry Hanratty — he left with a shoulder separation.

80. Bubba Smith

81. Rod Sherman

82. Terry Hanratty against Purdue in 1967 — 63 (completed 29)

83. "What tho the odds
    Be great or small
    Notre Dame men
    Will win over all!"

84. Forty-five minutes in the two previous years

85. 1972

86. Jim Seymour — 13 (276 yards) against Purdue in 1966

87. Gator Bowl against Penn State or Georgia in 1971

88. The 4–4 defense utilized by Ara Parseghian

89. The recognition of best performances in each game by a defensive back, linebacker, lineman, offensive back and offensive lineman. Great plays were noted by painting blue stars on the gold helmets.

90. He played defensive back Nick Rassas as a receiver. Rassas caught a touchdown pass at the end of the game against Wisconsin and said, "Oh, God, how I've dreamed of that."

91. Johnny Lattner — he led his team during his career in four offensive and defensive categories as well as performing punting and punt return duties.

92. Once — the last game of the 1972 season against USC and the 1973 Orange Bowl against Nebraska

93. Steve Niehaus, in 1972

94. Bill Etter, 146 yards (11 attempts) against Navy in 1969

95. Twenty-nine, with six coming in the 1966 season

96. Joe Theisman (1970), John Huarte (1964), and Bob Williams (1949) — all with 16

97. Marchy Schwartz (1930) 927 yards, Creighton Miller (1943) 911 yards, Neil Worden (1953) 859 yards, Wayne Bullock (1974) 855 yards and George Gipp (1920) 827 yards

98. Thirty-one

99. Mike Johnston 13 (1982)

100. Vagas Ferguson, 255 yards on 30 carries against Georgia Tech in 1978

101. In 1986 Tim Brown totaled 1,937 yards (254 rushing, 910 receiving, 698 kickoff returns and 75 punt returns).

102. John Carney

103. Joe Heap — 71 career receptions
     (Jim Seymour — 138 receptions)

104. Bob Golic, a tri-captain in 1978, and Mike Golic, a tri-captain in 1984

105. Steven Beuerlein (1986)

106. 73 points against Haskell College in 1932

107. Don Shafer, University of Southern California, 60 yards (1986)

108. Kent State

109. William and Mary College (1969 to 1971), North Carolina State (1972 to 1975), New York Jets (1976), Arkansas (1977 to 1983) and Minnesota (1984 to 1985)

110. Left to right: Ralph Guglielmi, QB; Johnny Lattner, HB; Neil Worden, FB; and Joe Heap, HB

111. Number 57 has been worn by 27 players; numbers 97, 98 and 99 have been worn by five players each.

112. The Irish Guardsmen are a marching unit that accompanies the band during its game performance clad in kilts and bearskin shakos.

113. John Fyfe

HALFTIME

. . . shake down the thunder from the sky.

1. As a chemistry research assistant, Knute Rockne worked for the inventor of synthetic rubber. Who was he?

2. Where did Gus Dorais and Knute Rockne practice their forward passing during the summer vacation of 1913?

3. What impact did the ND win over Army in 1913 have on collegiate football?

4. ND has had many four- and some five-year players during periods of freshman eligibility. Two players at the turn of the century, however, had the distinction of playing six seasons. Name them.

5. Who was the coach of ND's first "Champions of the West" 1909 team?

6. How many games has ND lost to Ivy League teams?

7. Name three ND coaches who had better winning percentages than Rockne.

8. How many player-coaches have there been in ND history?

9. What is the longest fumble return in Irish history?

10. What team has the highest winning percentage in college football history (through 1986)?

11. How many seasons has ND been undefeated and untied, undefeated, or suffered only one loss?

12. Through 1986, ND has played 889 games. How many have been against Catholic college opponents?

13. What position did Frank Leahy play at ND?

14. What were the largest crowds to watch an ND game?

15. What was Horseman Jim Crowley's nickname?

16. What was Rockne's coaching record at ND?

17. What player, upon scoring the tying touchdown against Army, said, "That's one for the Gipper."

18. Who scored the winning touchdown against Army in 1928, the game of Rockne's "Gipper Speech"?

Boston Public Library, Print Department

19. Perhaps the artist who created the logo of the ND leprechaun had this man in mind. Who is he?

20. In 1926 ND was undefeated and untied for the first eight games, then lost to Carnegie Tech in an earthshaking upset. Who actually coached the Irish in that game?

21. This swift All-American halfback from Texas led the Irish offense immediately following the "Four Horsemen" era. Who was he?

22. Who holds the record for most kickoff returns in a game?

23. In the "Four Horsemen Game" against Army in 1924, Irish victory was assured only after a late-game interception by this ND center who was playing with two broken hands. Who was he?

24. Like the Beatles, the "Four Horsemen" backfield had an original cast member who was replaced early in his career. Who was he?

25. Who captained the 1927 national championship team?

26. What team broke ND's record of 93 consecutive games unbeaten at home?

27. Who were the archrival teams in Knute Rockne's novel *The Four Winners*?

28. What college team defeated Rockne-coached teams most often?

29 In what year did ND first play an eleven-game schedule?

30. Which of the Four Horsemen was first named All-American?

Notre Dame Sports Information Department

31. Name these players, the first black football monogram winners.

32. Did Knute Rockne ever play against Jim Thorpe?

33. What was the average weight of the Four Horsemen?

34. Who portrayed Knute Rockne in the film, *Knute Rockne, All American*?

35. How many sons of head coaches played at ND?

36. Who did the punting in the scenes featuring George Gipp in the movie?

37. Leon Hart was one of only two linemen to win the Heisman Trophy. Who was the other?

38. Which of the Four Horsemen eventually became head coach at ND?

39. Legend has it that this 1934 All-American center

kicked off and caught his own kick without the ball touching the ground. Who was he?

40. In the famous 18–13 comeback victory over Ohio State in 1935, with the Buckeyes leading, 13–12, and less than two minutes to play, Irish hero of the day, Andy Pilney, tackled running back Dick Belz so hard that he lost the ball to an alert ND defender. Name that defender.

41. Elmer Layden's coaching career at ND was highlighted by many close games. Of the 63 games he coached, how many were decided by seven points or less?

42. What other famous football coach was portrayed by Pat O'Brien on film?

43. What campus facility bears a football term as its identification?

44. Which head coach and university president were the only pair to serve concurrently?

45. What former All-American lineman was assistant director in the film *Knute Rockne, All-American*?

46. Which ND player was the only leading team rusher four years in a row?

47. Who was the first recipient of the Outland Trophy (college's best interior lineman)?

48. The 1949 ND-SMU game was highlighted by a little known SMU halfback subbing for

All-American Doak Walker. He nearly spoiled the Irish's fourth consecutive unbeaten season. Who was he?

49. This meeting signifies a change of attitude towards football and its importance to the growth of ND as a university. What is happening?

50. In 1950 what Purdue quarterback led his team to a 28–14 victory over ND, snapping the Irish 39-game unbeaten streak?

51. Despite his end-of-game defensive heroics, what were Johnny Lujack's offensive statistics in the 1946 0–0 tie with Army?

52. This great Leahy-era end (1949 to 1951) became one of John Unitas's favorite receivers when he starred for the Baltimore Colts. Who was he?

53. In 1947 Army had gone unbeaten for 34 straight games. What team beat West Point before the Irish had the chance to seek revenge?

54. What ND player holds the record for the longest run from scrimmage?

55. The 1947 team was considered the deepest in talent. How many players from that team went on to pro ball?

56. Who was the captain of the 1946 national championship team?

57. What ND All-American end scored over 400 points in the pros without scoring a touchdown?

58. How many times has an ND team been ranked number one in the country in total offense?

59. What ND player won a monogram at three different positions?

60. Name the members of Army's "Powerhouse" backfield of 1945 and 1946.

61. What were the uniform numbers of the six ND Heisman Trophy winners?

62. ND has had 67 NCAA consensus All-Americans. What number most frequently adorned these players?

63. ND has been shut out (loss or tie) 68 times. What opponent has accomplished this most often?

64. ND has had two players named Rockne. Name them.

University of Notre Dame, Sports Information Department

65. This athlete won the Heisman Trophy over such players as Jim Brown, Len Dawson, Jim Parker (all members of the Pro Football Hall of Fame) and John Brodie. Who is he?

66. Who were team captains the last time ND played Indiana?

67. Nine of ten game- and career-passing records by an ND opponent are held by quarterbacks at one school. Name it.

68. Who kicked the field goal to beat Army, 23–21, in 1957?

69. This All-American tackle from 1960 starred for many years as an All-Pro for the Pittsburgh Steelers. Name him.

70. How many times has ND led the nation in total defense?

71. Prior to ND's contests with Boston College – in the regular season in 1975 and the Liberty Bowl in 1983 – what team was ND's last Catholic college opponent?

72. How many head football coaches has ND had?

73. Name the brother duo of the 1970s who made All-American honors at ND.

74. Who was ND's first black captain?

75. Who holds the record for most pass completions in a season?

76. What professional team drafted Joe Theismann in 1971?

77. In 1970 this Irish placekicker's clutch field goal with only 2:54 remaining led ND to a 3–0 victory over LSU. Name him.

78. What was the nickname given to LSU's stingy defensive unit that year?

79. How long was Ara Parseghian's best unbeaten streak?

University of Notre Dame, Sports Information Department

80. Name this All-American end who led the Irish in scoring in 1957 and 1958.

81. Who holds the ND record for most interceptions in a season?

82. What is ND's single-game high for first downs?

83. Only two defensive tackles have been named consensus All-Americans. Name them.

84. What ND football coach's high school yearbook predicted his ultimately being head coach at ND?

85. This consensus 1969 All-American tackle was voted UPI's lineman of the year. Who was he?

86. What coach first used Moreau Seminary as a "night before game" dormitory for the team?

87. Who was the University of Texas's answer to the Gipper at the 1970 Cotton Bowl?

88. What 1969 Second Team All-American center won a Rhodes Scholarship?

89. When was the last pep rally held in the old fieldhouse?

90. Who said, "Not even the Pope would vote ND number one"?

91. This Irish lineman's team-leading 97 tackles in 1971 earned him First Team All-American status. Name him.

92. What player's father was given the distinct privilege of running through the tunnel to the field with the team?

93. In what year did ND go scoreless at home?

94. Of ND's 67 consensus All-Americans, which position has produced the most selections?

Notre Dame Sports Information Department

95. Name these members of the ND squad who broke the longest winning streak in college football history.

96. What is the highest national rank in passing achieved by an ND team?

97. Who holds the record for the longest field goal in ND history?

98. Who was the first running back to gain 1,000 yards in one season?

99. Who holds the Irish record for the most 100-yard rushing games in a career?

100. Which former ND coach never finished in the AP top twenty?

101. Which two ND runners have rushed for 200 yards per game twice in one season?

102. Who are the only Irish linemen to win the coveted Vince Lombardi Trophy?

103. Which ND football coach had the best Bowl record for more than one game?

104. Who holds the record for the longest interception return?

105. One of quarterback Joe Montana's patented miracles occurred on October 18, 1975, with ND's 31–30 thriller over Air Force. What was the score when the fireworks began?

106. During one of his drives downfield, Montana was intercepted by Air Force's Jim Miller, who then fumbled on ND's 35 yard line. Who recovered the fumble for the Irish?

107. Who scored the third and final touchdown for ND with 3:21 remaining in the game?

108. Who kicked the winning extra point?

109. Air Force, in a final attempt to move the ball upfield, had a pass broken up on fourth and ten from their own 46. Who was the Irish defender?

University of Notre Dame, Sports Information Department

110. This player later became a key member of the famous "No-Name" defense of the Miami Dolphins. Who is he?

111. Who holds the record for total yards on kickoff returns in a season?

112. What player position has produced the most captains?

HALFTIME — ANSWERS

1. Professor Julius A. Nieuwland, C.S.C.

2. Cedar Point, Ohio, a resort on Lake Erie

3. It carried the popularity of the forward pass to the East, where collegiate football was dominant.

4. Jack Mullen (1894–1899) and George Lins (1896–1901)

5. Shorty Longman, the first of Fielding Yost's pupils to defeat the legendary Yost

6. One – to Yale in 1914

7. John L. Marks (13-0-2), .933; Thomas Barry (12-1-1), .893; Victor M. Place (8-1-0), .889

8. Three: James L. Morison (1894), H. G. Hadden (1895) and Frank E. Hering (1896)

9. Frank Shaughnessy, 107 yards against Kansas in 1904 (on a 110-yard field)

10. Notre Dame (651–198–40) .755

11. 46 out of 98: undefeated and untied — 11; undefeated — 10; one loss — 25

12. In 24 games against 13 different Catholic college opponents, ND's record is 21-0-3.

13. Tackle

14. 120,000 on 11/26/27 at Soldiers Field, Chicago, when ND beat USC, 7–6; and 120,000 on 10/13/28 at Soldiers Field, Chicago, when ND beat Navy, 7–0

15. "Sleepy Jim"

16. 105–12–5 (1918 to 1930) .881

17. Jack Chevigny, in the 1928 Army game

18. Johnny "One Play" O'Brien, on a diving pass reception from halfback Johnny Niemiec — O'Brien rarely played either before or after this game.

19. Coach Frank Leahy

20. Hunk Anderson — Rockne was in Chicago scout-

ing the Army-Navy game. Navy was to be on the ND schedule the following year for the first time.

21. Christie Flanagan (1925–1927)

22. George Gipp had eight against Army for 157 yards in 1920.

23. Adam Walsh, team captain

24. The injured fullback, Paul Castner, was replaced by Elmer Layden in the 1922 Carnegie Tech game.

25. John "Clipper" Smith

26. Carnegie Tech beat ND 27-7 on November 17, 1928, the first defeat at home since 1905.

27. Dulac (Notre Dame Du Lac) and Aksarben (Nebraska spelled backwards)

28. Nebraska — three times: 1922, 1923 and 1925

29. 1921, under Knute Rockne, 10–1–0

30. Don Miller in his junior year

31. Dick Washington (number 41) and Wayne Edmonds (number 82)

32. Once as a pro in Canton, Ohio, in 1916

33. 158 pounds

34. Pat O'Brien

35. Three: Jim Leahy, 1968; Mike Parseghian, 1974; and Skip Holtz, 1986

36. Jim Thorpe

37. Larry Kelley, Yale University (1936)

38. Elmer Layden (1934 to 1940) 47–13–3, .770

39. Jack Robinson (1932 to 1934)

40. Second-string center Henry Pojman

41. Thirty-two — he won 22, tied 3 and lost only 7.

42. Frank Cavanaugh, "The Iron Major," who coached at Holy Cross, Boston College and Fordham

43. The "Huddle"

44. Elmer Layden and John F. O'Hara, C.S.C., 1934 to 1940

45. Jesse Hibbs (USC 1926–1928)

46. Emil Sitko (1946 through 1949)

47. George Connor, 1946

48. Kyle Rote — ND hung on to a narrow 27–20 victory.

49. Third-year president Rev. Theodore M. Hesburgh, C.S.C., turns over the head-coaching reins

from Frank Leahy to a youthful Terry Brennan in 1954.

50. Dale Samuels

51. Five completions in 17 attempts, with four interceptions

52. Jim Mutscheller

53. Columbia, 21–20, in a major upset

54. Bob Livingstone (against USC in 1947) 92 yards

55. Forty-two

56. There was a new captain each game.

57. Jim Martin (1946–1949), placekicker for the Detroit Lions and Washington Redskins

58. Twice: 1946 and 1949

59. Marty Wendell (1944 and 1946 to 1948) – fullback, guard and center

60. Arnold Tucker, Felix "Doc" Blanchard, Glenn Davis and Tom Williams

61. Bertelli – 48, Lujack – 32, Hart – 82, Lattner – 14, Hornung – 5, Huarte – 7

62. Numbers 5, 14, 32, 81 and 85 (each worn by three players)

63. Army has done it eight times: 1922 (T), 1925, 1927, 1931, 1941 (T), 1944, 1945 and 1946 (T).

64. Knute Rockne and Rockne Morrissey

65. Paul Hornung

66. Al Ecuyer and Chuck Puntillo (1958)

67. Purdue

68. Monty Stickles (his first attempt ever!)

69. Myron Pottios

70. Twice: in 1946 and 1974

71. The University of Detroit in 1951

72. Twenty-five

73. Larry DiNardo (1969, 1970) and Gerry DiNardo (1974)

74. Tom Gatewood, 1971

75. Joe Theismann (1970) — 155 (attempted 268)

76. Miami Dolphins, fourth round, 99th pick overall

77. Scott Hempel

78. "The Chinese Bandits"

79. Twelve (1965 to 1967)

80. Monty Stickles

81. Mike Townsend, ten (1972)

82. Thirty-six against Army in 1974

83. Mike McCoy (1969) and Greg Marx (1972)

84. Ara Parseghian

85. Mike McCoy

86. Ara Parseghian

87. Freddie Steinmark, a Texas football player whose leg had been amputated

88. Mike Oriard

89. 1969

90. Bob Devaney, Nebraska coach, after his 1971 victory over LSU in the Orange Bowl

91. Mike Kadish (1969 to 1971)

92. Pat Dinardo, father of Larry and Gerry

93. 1933: four games

94. End (including tight end and split end): 12

95. Left to right: Dick Lynch, Jim Schaaf, Nick Pietrosante and Coach Terry Brennan from the 1957 team that defeated Oklahoma, 7–0

96. Fifth (in 1954 and 1964)

97. Dave Reeve (Pittsburgh, 1976): 53 yards

98. Al Hunter who gained 1,058 yards in 1976

99. Allen Pinkett, 21 (1982 to 1985)

100. Gerry Faust

101. Jim Stone (1980) and Vagas Ferguson (1978)

102. Defensive end Walt Patukski in 1971, and defensive end Ross Browner in 1977

103. Dan Devine, 3-1-0

104. Luther Bradley ran one back 99 yards against Purdue in 1975.

105. At 13:40 of the final period, the Air Force was ahead, 30-10.

106. Offensive tackle Pat Pohlen

107. Jerome Heavens

108. Dave Reeve

109. Left cornerback Tom Lopienski

110. Nick Buoniconti

111. Tim Brown (1986), 698 yards

112. End — 22 captains; the guard position is next with 20 captains.

THIRD QUARTER
. . . What though the odds be great or small?

1. ND has had two seasons in its 100-year collegiate football history in which the team did not play. When?

2. Who captained the 1913 undefeated, untied ND team that shocked the football world by beating Army in its first meeting?

3. What was the final score of the famous 1913 ND-Army game in which the Gus Dorais and Knute Rockne passer-receiver tandem popularized the forward pass?

4. What ND running back once held the world record in the 40-, 50- and 60-yard dashes?

5. Although Dorais and Rockne popularized the forward pass in 1913, when was the forward pass instituted in the rules of football?

6. Who holds the ND record for most points scored in a single game?

University of Notre Dame, Sports Information Department

7. In spite of a virtual one-year career, this Heisman Trophy winning quarterback still holds eight game, season and career records in passing and total offense. Who is he?

8. Who was ND's first quarterback?

9. What is the all-time longest punt return by an Irish back in a game without scoring a touchdown?

10. Who was the first ND center to be chosen All-American?

11. What was the longest kickoff return in ND history without a touchdown being scored?

12. How many coaches have coached 11-game seasons?

13. An NCAA record category recognizes All-Americans selected on a unanimous basis. ND has had the most with 23 selections. Which school is next?

14. What are the "Hering Awards"?

15. What was the "Power House Special"?

16. Who leads ND in career punt-return yardage?

17. What ND coach had the most undefeated and untied seasons?

18. In what year did ND play all its games away?

19. What was Knute Rockne's last win?

20. Who was the brilliant quarterback during Rockne's era who made 14 First Team All-Americans in two years?

21. "Jumping Joe" Savoldi, the star fullback of Rockne's last team of 1930, was dismissed from the team for an infraction that would be unnoticed today. What was this infraction?

22. In 1930 what incident hit the newspapers after the Penn game that compounded Savoldi's problems and forced him to leave school?

23. What sport did Savoldi enter after ND?

24. What famous ND halfback in the late 1920s carried the nickname of a famous comic-strip character of the era?

25. What All-American Irish tackle became the head of one of the largest corporations in the U.S.?

26. Who is known as the first of a string of famous ND "Watch Charm" guards?

27. What was the *New York Daily News* sports page headline after the "Gipper" victory over Army in 1928?

28. Who was the coach of the team in 1929 during Rockne's absence caused by phlebitis?

29. What was the name of the first book written and published by Knute Rockne?

30. What campus construction was funded from the earnings of ND's Rose Bowl appearance in 1925?

University of Notre Dame, Sports Information Department

31. Ara Parseghian produced the most potent offensive teams in ND football history. What was the team's average point per game production during the "Era of Ara"?

32. This All-American is considered by many to have been the greatest center to have played under Knute Rockne. Name him.

33. Who was the All-American roving guard from the Rockne era who played without a helmet?

34. In what year did ND first have co-captains?

35. The 1929 unbeaten, untied Irish season was preserved when this fleet ND halfback intercepted an Army pass and ran 96 yards to beat Army 7–0 in the last game of the season. Who was he?

36. Since Associated Press polling began in 1936, ND has won seven national championships, more than any other school. What college is second?

37. How many ND captains were consensus All-Americans in the year of their captaincy?

38. Who played "mythical" players in the 1931 film, *The Spirit of Notre Dame*?

39. This All-American guard later was head coach at the University of Indiana. Name him.

40. Who holds the ND record for the longest punt in a game?

41. What 1938 All-American end coached an NCAA championship basketball team?

42. This consensus All-American end blocked kicks in two consecutive games in 1937 to win two tough ones for the Irish. Who was he?

43. In 1925 Knute Rockne actually signed a contract to coach at another college. Can you name it?

University of Notre Dame, Sports Information Department

44. He was a member of ND's first defensive front four when college football returned to the two-platoon system in 1964. Who is he?

45. Surprisingly, the first genuine sports hero at ND did not play football, but baseball. Who was he?

46. The 1896 head football coach, Francis E. Hering, became widely known as the "Father of _____." Complete the phrase.

47. ND lost one game in 1948. To whom?

48. Who succeeded Johnny Lujack at quarterback?

49. Who captained the 1947 national championship team?

50. What was the worst defeat under Frank Leahy?

51. Frank Leahy's least productive team produced two First Team All-Americans. Who were they?

52. On the brink of an upset loss to USC in 1948, what ND back endeared himself to Irish fans forever with an 87-yard kickoff return with 2:35 left to set up a 14–14 tie and keep his team's unbeaten streak intact?

53. How many times has an ND team been ranked number one in the country in rushing?

54. ND has played in all kinds of weather: snow, sleet and rain. But can you remember when they played during an earthquake?

55. Who kicked the extra point in the closing seconds of the game to tie USC in 1948 to preserve ND's unbeaten stretch?

University of Notre Dame, Sports Information Department

56. This member of ND's first two-platoon front four continued his career as a "Purple People-Eater." Who is he?

57. ND students have celebrated football victories at many South Bend food and drink emporiums. Which was the first?

58. How many times has ND led the nation in total offensive yards per game?

59. He was an All-American guard on the 1945 and 1946 teams and one of the first men in football to wear contact lenses. Who was he?

60. What is the current capacity of ND Stadium?

61. What is the MacArthur Bowl?

62. Who controls the "rights" to "The ND Victory March"?

63. What was the longest losing streak in ND history?

64. In modern times, only one game has been cancelled. When was it?

65. In 1961, the centennial year of the Civil War, the Irish fielded "Yankee" and "Rebel" co-captains. Who were they?

66. When was the last time Army defeated the Irish?

67. When was the last year that ND players wore leather helmets?

68. Although the 1957 ND-Army game was settled by a dramatic field goal, who was the All-American selected as the outstanding player of the game?

69. This talented halfback of the Terry Brennan years was a track All-American in 1958. Who was he?

70. How many times have ND teams been on both ends of opponents' winning or unbeaten streaks?

71. ND has many players enshrined in the National Football Foundation Hall of Fame, but can you name the five coaches who are enshrined?

Notre Dame, Sports Information Department

72. Name these members of the 1966 national championship backfield who all went on to play pro football.

73. Name the only two men who served as player, assistant coach and head coach at ND.

74. What change in university administration allowed participation in Bowls?

75. How many All-Americans did Ara Parseghian coach in his 11 years at ND?

76. What was the score of Ara Parseghian's last victory?

77. What was the worst defeat of Ara Parseghian's ND career?

78. What was the "Mirror Defense"?

79. Who holds the record for most pass attempts in a season?

80. Both defensive tackles on the 1974 ND squad earned First Team All-American status. Can you name them?

81. Name the passing combination for the two-point play culminating in an 8–7 Irish win over the Boilermakers in 1971.

82. How many times has an ND team been ranked number one in the country in rushing defense?

83. When this consensus All-American linebacker graduated, he was replaced by Bob Crable, who garnered those honors twice. Who was he?

84. In what year did ND play two Bowl games?

85. Who is the only ND player to win the Walter Camp award?

86. Who was the first ND linebacker to earn First Team All-American honors?

87. This defensive back still holds the ND record for highest average yards returned per interception. Who was he?

88. What was the best total offensive production in a game under Ara Parseghian?

89. What players made up the backfield of ND's most prolific total-offense season?

University of Notre Dame, Sports Information Department

90. From right to left, this trio combined their efforts on countless scoring plays.

91. Who said, "If ND were playing Russia tomorrow, I'd be right out there waving the old hammer and sickle"?

92. Name the seven opponents to defeat the Irish in Ara Parseghian's career.

93. Which ND coaches always finished in the Associated Press top twenty?

94. Since 1888, when ND tallied 30 points in a three-game season, what team has the least points in a season?

95. ND had three two-time Academic All-Americans. Name them.

96. How many ND players had such distinguished pro careers to warrant enshrinement in the Pro Football Hall of Fame?

97. How many ND backs have rushed for over 1,000 yards in a season?

98. In what game did coach Dan Devine boost the spirit of the players by having the team wear green jerseys for the first time in a dozen years?

99. What film was shown to players the Friday night before that game?

100. Although ND lost to USC, 27–25, in 1978 on a 37-yard field goal with four seconds left, the Irish under Joe Montana overcame a wide deficit to actually take the lead. What was the score at the end of three periods?

101. Luther Bradley holds the ND record for most interceptions in a career with 17. Whose record did he break?

102. Who holds the ND record for most career fumble recoveries?

University of Notre Dame, Sports Information Department

103. This great ND offensive lineman went on to play in more Super Bowls than any ND player in NFL history.

104. Name the only First Team All-American offensive tackle during the Dan Devine era.

105. In the 1979 ND-South Carolina game, the Irish were trailing, 17–3, late in the third quarter when they battled back to win, 18–17. Who threw the final touchdown pass and winning two-point conversion for ND?

106. How much time was left when the final touchdown pass was thrown?

107. Who caught the final 14-yard touchdown pass?

108. Who caught the clinching two-point conversion?

109. Earlier, with a little less than two minutes to play and South Carolina moving to the ND 41-yard line, Heisman winner George Rogers was stopped for no gain, forcing the Gamecocks to punt. Who stopped him?

110. Who captained the 1977 national championship team?

111. Name this offensive lineman of the 1980s who earned All-American accolades at two different positions.

112. Contrary to traditional opinion, ND coaches have not come from "the Notre Dame family" quite as often as perceived. Alumni have coached a total of 492 games, while non-alumni have coached a total of 386 games. Which has the greater winning percentage?

University of Notre Dame, Sports Information Department

113. Through 1986 this great pass receiver still holds eight game, season and career pass-receiving records. Who is he?

THIRD QUARTER — ANSWERS

1. 1890 and 1891

2. Knute Rockne

3. ND won, 35–13.

4. Arthur "Dutch" Bergman

5. 1906

6. Art Smith scored 35 (seven five-point touch-downs) against Loyola in 1911.

7.　John Huarte

8.　George Cartier (1887)

9.　95 yards — Harry "Red" Miller against Olivet in 1909 (110-yard field)

10.　Frank Rydzewski (1917)

11.　Alfred "Dutch" Bergman — 105 yards against Loyola in 1911 (110-yard field)

12.　Rockne, 1921; Leahy, 1942; Parseghian, 1974; Devine, 1975 to 1980; Faust, 1981 to 1985; and Holtz, 1986

13.　The University of Southern California with 20 picks

14.　Awards presented to outstanding performers in the annual Blue-Gold game, named after former ND head coach Frank Hering (1896–1898)

15.　An alumni train from Chicago whose terminus on the ND and Western tracks was the depot at the campus power house

16.　Frank Carideo — 947 yards (1928 to 1930)

17.　Knute Rockne — five: 1919, 1920, 1924, 1929, 1930

18.　1929, during construction of the stadium

19.　December 6, 1930, when ND beat USC, 27–0

20. Frank Carideo (1929 and 1930)

21. Against university rules, he got married secretly.

22. "Joe Savoldi Sues for Divorce"

23. He became one of the most successful professional wrestlers of all time.

24. Larry "Moon" Mullins (1927–1929)

25. Fred Miller (1928) became president of Miller Brewery.

26. John "Clipper" Smith

27. "Gipp's Ghost Beats Army"

28. Tom Lieb

29. *The Four Winners* in 1925

30. The addition to the field house housing the new basketball floor and stadia

31. 30.61 points per game, higher than any coach since John L. Marks (1911 and 1912)

32. Art "Bud" Boeringer (1925–1926)

33. Jack Cannon (1929)

34. 1926 — Gene Edwards and Tom Hearden

35. Jack Elder

36. Oklahoma and Alabama — each have won five.

37. Twenty-two — the first was Eddie Anderson, and the last was John Scully in 1980.

38. Lew Ayres as "Bucky O'Brien" and Andy Devine as "Truck McCall"

39. Bernie Crimmins (1939–1941)

40. Bill Shakespeare, 86 yards against Pitt in 1935

41. Earl Brown (1936–1938) led Dartmouth to the 1944 NCAA championship.

42. Chuck Sweeney (1935–1937) against Navy and Minnesota

43. Columbia University. ND asserted that it would not stand in Rockne's way, but he had second thoughts and stayed in South Bend.

44. Tom Regner

45. Adrian "Cap" Anson, a member of the Baseball Hall of Fame

46. Mother's Day

47. They lost to the "old-timers" in their annual spring game, 20–14.

48. Frank Tripucka in 1948

49. George Connor

50. The loss to Michigan State, 35–0, in 1951

51. Bob Williams and Jerry Groom (1950)

52. Bill Gay

53. Once, 1946

54. 1948 at the University of Southern California

55. Steve Oracko

56. Alan Page

57. Hullie & Mike's, 112 South Michigan Street, the first in a long line including Sweeney's, The Philadelphia, Howard Park Tavern, Joer's, Guiseppe's, Frankie's, Fat Wally's and The Electric Beer Joint

58. Three: 1943 (418 yards), 1946 (441 yards) and 1949 (435 yards)

59. John "Cut" Mastrangelo (1944–1946)

60. 59,075

61. The award presented by the National Football Foundation Hall of Fame (NFFHF), since 1959, to the national champion

62. Paul McCartney, through the ex-Beatle's publishing company, MPL Communications, Inc.

63. Eight in 1960, under Joe Kuharich

64. The game against Iowa on November 23, 1963, the day after John F. Kennedy's assassination

65. The Yankee was Nick Buoniconti of Springfield, Massachusetts, and the Rebel was Norb Roy of Baton Rouge, Louisiana.

66. 1958, the year Army's Pete Dawkins won the Heisman Trophy

67. 1958

68. Fullback Nick Pietrosante

69. Aubrey Lewis

70. Three: USC (23 games), Oklahoma (47 games) and Army (25 games)

71. Knute Rockne was enshrined in 1951, Frank Leahy in 1970, Jesse Harper in 1971, Ara Parseghian in 1980, and Dan Devine in 1985.

72. Left to right: Rocky Bleier, Larry Conjar, Nick Eddy and Terry Hanratty

73. Knute Rockne and Hunk Anderson

74. A new academic calendar, changing the scheduling of final exams from after the Christmas holidays to before

75. Parseghian coached 51 All-Americans (First or Second Team) from 1964 through 1974.

76. ND beat Alabama, 13–11, in the Orange Bowl, on January 1, 1975.

77. USC's 55–24 victory on November 30, 1974, the game in which USC scored 49 points in 17 minutes — the game was Parseghian's last regular-season game as head coach.

78. A defense Ara Parseghian devised to neutralize the "Wishbone Offense" of Texas in the 1971 Cotton Bowl, ending the Longhorns' 30-game winning streak

79. Joe Theismann, 1970, 268 (completed 155)

80. Mike Fanning and Steve Niehaus

81. Quarterback Pat Steenberge to tight end Mike Creaney. Creaney purposely slipped to one knee, then got up and caught the pass on what has now become known as the "genuflect play."

82. Once, in 1974

83. Bob Golic

84. 1973 — the Orange Bowl on January 1, 1973, against Nebraska, and the Sugar Bowl on December 31, 1973, against Alabama

85. Tight end Ken McAfee (1977)

86. Jim Carroll — in 1964 he earned the honors from *Sporting News*, *Time* and the *Football News*.

87. Ralph Stepaniak (1969, 1970 and 1971) 13.8 yards

88. 720 yards against Navy in 1969

89. Joe Theismann, Ed Gulyas, Denny Allen and Bill Barz — in 1970 they gained 5,105 yards.

90. Quarterback Terry Hanratty, split end Jim Seymour and the legendary "Touchdown Jesus"

91. The sports editor of *The Baton Rouge Newspaper* before the 1970 LSU game

92. USC, Purdue, Michigan State, Texas, LSU, Missouri and Nebraska

93. Ara Parseghian (11 years) and Ed McKeever (one year)

94. The 1933 team scored 32 points in nine games — they were shut out six times.

95. Joe Restic (1977 and 1978), Greg Marx (1971 and 1972) and Tom Gatewood (1970 and 1971)

96. Five: George Connor (Chicago Bears), Paul Hornung (Green Bay Packers), Earl "Curley" Lambeau (Green Bay Packers), Wayne Millner (Boston and Washington Redskins) and George Trafton

97. Three: Al Hunter (1976); Vagas Ferguson (1978 and 1979); and Allen Pinkett (1983, 1984 and 1985)

98. ND's 49–19 victory over USC on October 22, 1977, Dan Devine's only victory over USC in six years

99. *Rocky*

100. USC was ahead, 24–6.

101. Tom MacDonald (1961–1963)

102. Ross Browner — 12

103. Bob Kuechenberg, Miami Dolphins

104. Tim Foley, 1979

105. Quarterback Rusty Lisch

106. Forty-two seconds

107. Tight end Dean Masztak

108. Flanker Pete Holohan

109. Linebacker Bob Crable; he made 24 tackles that day.

110. There were three captains: Ross Browner, Terry Eurick and Willie Fry

111. Larry Williams, offensive tackle (Third Team, *Football News*) in 1983, and guard (Second Team, UPI; Third Team, AP and *Football News*) in 1984

112. The non-alumni coaches have a .768 percentage, while the alumni coaches have a .751 percentage.

113. Tom Gatewood

FOURTH QUARTER
. . . old Notre Dame will win over all . . .

1. What future head of state was a member of the Army team of 1913?

2. Who preceded Knute Rockne as head football coach?

3. What school record in another sport did Knute Rockne once hold while at ND?

4. After whom was Cartier Field named?

5. What was the capacity of Cartier Field, home of Irish football before Notre Dame Stadium?

6. What season produced the highest ND team scoring margin per game?

7. Name the only football player to earn four monograms in one year—twice.

8. What major rule change preceded the 1913 season when ND first played and upset Army?

9. How many substitues played in the 1913 Army game?

10. Besides "Irish," what other nicknames has ND competed under?

11. How many times has ND played in Yankee Stadium?

University of Notre Dame, Sports Information Department

12. He has been ND's only number-one pick in the NFL draft. Name him.

13. Who portrayed Jim Crowley of Four Horsemen fame in the movie, *Knute Rockne, All-American*?

14. The backfield of the 1930 national championship team was called better than the Four Horsemen. Who were the players?

15. When was the dedication of Notre Dame Stadium?

16. What ND football coach had an automobile named for him?

17. What was the record of Rockne's last team in 1930?

18. Who captained the 1929 national championship team?

19. Who was the University of Pennsylvania transfer who ran wild against his old team in an ND romp of 60–20 in 1930?

20. What season was Rockne's poorest?

21. Through an ingenious method of signal-calling, Rockne-coached teams rarely needed this time-consuming activity. Name it.

22. In the 1920 ND-Army game, the two opposing kickers, George Gipp and Red Reeder, participated in some pre-game psychological warfare. What were the results?

23. In ND's 12–6 victory over Army in 1928 (the "Gipper Game") the Cadets fought to the Irish one

yard line when time ran out. Name the great two-way Army back who nearly led his team to victory.

24. Who played in the starting backfield of the 1927 national champions, "The Forgotten Men"?

25. Name these teammates who became consensus All-Americans in successive years.

26. What were the uniform numbers of the "Four Horsemen"?

27. Who was ND's opponent in the first game at the stadium?

28. What was one ND coach's antidote to superstition for his players?

29. In 1924, the year of the "Four Horsemen", all but one was a consensus All-American. Who was he?

30. Who converted Knute Rockne to Catholicism?

31. What former ND tackle was the first head coach of the Air Force Academy?

32. What was the result of the last game Knute Rockne actually coached?

33. Where did Rockne live in South Bend?

34. What was the cost of construction of the Notre Dame Stadium in 1930?

35. How many unanimous national championships has ND won?

36. What relative of Knute Rockne also had a long career at ND?

37. Who portrayed Bonnie Rockne in the film *Knute Rockne, All-American*?

38. What incident at ND in 1940 precipitated the hiring of Frank Leahy as head coach?

39. What was the worst defeat under Hunk Anderson?

Notre Dame, Sports Information Department

40. This starting quarterback was replaced by ND's winningest career quarterback.

41. After running 70 yards a couple of plays earlier, Irish fullback Mario Tonelli scored the winning touchdown to beat the University of Southern California 13–6 with 1:45 left on November 27, 1937. What greater heights of heroism would Tonelli reach five years later?

42. Until ND beat Rose-Bowl-bound Army, 13–12, in the last game of the 1933 season, Army had held its opponents to only 13 points all season. How many points had ND scored in its previous eight games?

43. Prior to the Leprechaun, what was the ND mascot?

44. What distinction has been bestowed upon ND's marching band?

45. In addition to the "Victory March," there are three other school football songs. Can you name them?

46. Frank Leahy introduced a new formation in 1949 that became widely used. What was it?

47. What was Frank Leahy's record in 1953, his last season as head coach?

48. Who was captain of Frank Leahy's last football team at ND?

49. Who kicked the extra point with only 30 seconds left to tie Iowa, 14–14, in 1953 and preserve ND's undefeated season?

50. Who scored the touchdown?

51. Who threw the pass?

52. Who faked an injury with no timeouts left to allow ND to score its first touchdown in the same game?

53. What two other ND players followed suit later in the game?

University of Notre Dame, Sports Information Department

54. This Irish quarterback won more games at his position than any other but never achieved consensus All-American honors.

55. From 1946 through 1949, ND's record was
     36–0–2 and the team claimed three national
     championships. Name the five four-year mono-
     gram winners from this period who never played
     in a losing game.

56. Name the three other players who earned three
     monograms but were on the squad for all four
     years.

57. How many times did a Frank Leahy-coached team
     suffer consecutive losses?

58. Trailing 20–6 in the final period against Iowa in
     1951, ND came back to tie the Hawkeyes with 55
     seconds left on the extra-point conversion of a
     virtually unknown sophomore halfback. Who was
     he?

59. ND has been involved in many college football
     firsts, including the first TV broadcast from the
     West Coast to the rest of the country. When?

60. When did ND play its first night game?

61. What ND players have collected the most pieces
     of "hardware" in postseason awards, i.e. Heisman,
     Outland, Maxwell, Camp and Lombardi awards
     or trophies?

62. In addition to the six Heisman Trophy winners,
     ND has had two players finish second and five
     finish third. Can you name them?

63. ND had one three-time academic All-American.
     Name him.

64. Who co-captained the 1961 team and later became an All-Pro and Super Bowl linebacker?

65. Name the only ND Heisman Trophy winner who was not a consensus All-American.

66. When was the last time Navy defeated ND?

67. Who was the first kicking specialist to lead the team for a season in scoring?

68. This end was named to First Team All-American teams two consecutive years during the Joe Kuharich coaching years. Name him.

University of Notre Dame, Sports Information Department

69. Name this player, one of three ND recipients of the Outland Trophy.

70. This Irish back from the Kuharich years carried the ball 11 times for 176 yards (16 yards per carry!) against Oklahoma in 1961. Who was he?

71. What former ND player, while a professional for the New England Patriots, was called from the stands to play in a game?

72. Name the three Outland Trophy winners from ND.

73. Name two ND players who were two-sport All-Americans.

74. What were the most frequent player surnames in ND history?

75. He scored the most career touchdowns against ND. Who is he?

76. What typical act of Notre Dame spirit took place in 1964 when the team returned home after a season-ending loss to USC?

77. What great ND quarterback completed 33 of 58 passes for 526 yards and still lost to USC, 38–28?

78. Where did Ara Parseghian coach prior to ND?

79. Name the Michigan State coach whose football teams wreaked havoc with the Fighting Irish teams of the 1950s and 1960s.

University of Notre Dame, Sports Information Department

80. He is the first player to break George Gipp's rushing record of 2,341 yards, 58 years after it was established. Who is he?

81. During which "coaching era" were the greatest number of consensus All-Americans produced?

82. In 1975 this ND punter averaged 43.5 yards per punt for an ND season record. Name him.

83. In their 1973 Sugar Bowl game, an ND back recorded the longest kickoff return in Sugar Bowl history. What was his name?

84. Who was the first black All-American at ND?

85. Whom did the tall man in the black and white houndstooth hat ask for upon entering the ND locker room after the 1973 Sugar Bowl?

86. Who was Ara Parseghian's coach at Miami of Ohio?

87. After USC's 51–0 loss to the Irish in 1966, the Trojans' coach John McKay exacted a measure of revenge in 1967 when his team trounced ND, 24–7. Name his devastating offensive weapon.

88. Name the eight First Team All-Americans from the 1966 national champions.

89. Name the three Second Team All-Americans from that same team.

90. This talented halfback broke open the 1973 USC game with a spectacular 85-yard touchdown run. Name him.

91. Who threw the blocks breaking him loose?

92. The Irish 23–14 victory over USC in 1973 also broke a Trojan winning streak. How long was the streak?

93. Name the Irish defensive back who intercepted a Richard Todd pass on ND's 38 yard line with 68 seconds left to deny Alabama a national championship, 13–11, in the 1975 Orange Bowl.

94. Although Dave Casper garnered All-American

honors in 1973, the "other" end actually caught more passes and gained more yardage. Who was he?

95. What ND player "upset" Ara Parseghian by scoring a touchdown on a 72-yard punt return in a rout of Army in 1973?

96. In what season did female cheerleaders first appear?

97. Since 1967, when Rocky Bleier was captain, ND has had multiple captains each season until what player in 1986?

98. Who were the first female cheerleaders to "yell" for ND?

Notre Dame Sports Information Department

99. This quarterback, who holds only two of 60 passing or total-offense game, season or career records, still rates as one of the greatest in ND history.

100. Which ND coach had the most career losses?

101. Name this Chicago Bears star who holds the Irish record for most career punt returns.

102. Who owns the record for most career kickoff return yardage by an Irish player?

103. ND was the recipient of a $5,000 scholarship when Chevrolet picked this Irish tackle as its defensive player of the year in 1975. Who was he?

104. When did the practice of awarding numerals to freshmen players end?

105. Since ND began recording tackles made by line-men in 1956, who has been credited for most tackles ever in a season?

106. Who holds the ND record for most rushing yard-age in a season?

107. Trailing, 27–26, with four seconds left in this 1980 Michigan battle, a left-footed soccer-style kicker who had never kicked a field goal longer than 38 yards booted one for 51 yards into a 15 mile per hour wind for a 29–27 ND victory. Name him.

108. Who held the ball for the field goal attempt?

109. Who centered the crucial snap?

110. In that same game, with 42 seconds left, coach Dan Devine made a key decision to replace senior

quarterback Mike Coury with an untried freshman who could throw the long pass. Who was he?

111. Name the split end who caught this young quarterback's sideline pass and touched the sideline chalk
to set up the field goal.

112. Name the Irish cornerback who intercepted a
Michigan pass for a key touchdown in the third
quarter.

FOURTH QUARTER — ANSWERS

1. Dwight David Eisenhower

2. Jesse Harper

3. Indoor pole vault (12'4")

4. Warren A. Cartier, Class of 1877; he volunteered to purchase the land, supplied the lumber and constructed the grandstand.

5. 30,000

6. 1912 — 51.7 points

7. Arthur "Dutch" Bergman (1913–1914 and 1914–1915), football, baseball, basketball and track (11 total)

8. Team offensive possession increased from three downs to four downs.

9. One — Bunny Larkin

10. "Catholics" (in the 1800's) and "Ramblers" (early 1920s)

11. Twenty-four times

12. Walt Patulski

13. Nick Lukats, who later succeeded Jim Crowley in the ND backfield

14. Frank Carideo, QB; Marty Brill,RH; Joe Savoldi, FB; and Marchy Schwartz, LH

15. October 11, 1930

16. Knute Rockne — Studebaker manufactured about 30,000 "Rockne" cars in 1932 and 1933.

17. 10–0–0: national champs

18. John Law, RG

19. Marty Brill — he scored on touchdown runs of 66, 36 and 25 yards.

20. 1928 (5–4–0) — representing one third of Rockne's career losses. One of the wins, however, was the "Get one for the Gipper Game."

21. A huddle

22. They engaged in a kicking duel. Army kicker, Reeder, dropped out on the 40 yard line. Gipp walked to the 50, drop-kicked two over one cross-bar, then turned and kicked the other two over the other bar.

23. Chris Cagle

24. Charlie Riley, QB; Christie Flanagan, LH; Bucky Dahman, RH; and Elmer Wynne, FB

25. Dave Casper (1973) and Pete Demmerle (1974)

26. Harry Stuhldreher, number 32; Don Miller, number 16; Jim Crowley, number 8; and Elmer Layden, number 5

27. Southern Methodist in 1930

28. The number 13 was worn on Knute Rockne's jersey during practice.

29. Don Miller, halfback

30. Rev. Edward V. Mooney baptized Knute Rockne in 1925 in St. Edward's Hall.

31. Lawrence "Buck" Shaw

32. A loss to the New York Giants pro team in an exhibition to benefit the unemployed of New York, the city of his good friend, Mayor Jimmy Walker

33. 1006, St. Vincent's Street, South Bend (later on East Wayne Street)

34. Approximately $750,000

35. Five: 1930, 1943, 1949, 1966 and 1977

36. Joe Dierickx, Rock's brother-in-law, was the official stadium caretaker

37. Gale Page

38. Elmer Layden, his predecessor, became commissioner of the National Football League.

39. There were two 19–0 losses in 1933 — to Purdue and USC.

40. Cliff Brown

41. In April 1942, he would survive the infamous "Bataan Death March."

42. Nineteen

43. An Irish Terrier — the first was Brick-top Shaun Rhu, in 1930; he was followed by several dogs named Clashmore Mike and Shannon View Mike until the late sixties.

44. The ND band, which was started in 1845 and has played at every home game since 1887, was declared a "landmark of American music" by the National Music Council in 1976.

45. "Hike Notre Dame" (1924), "Down the Line" (1926) — music by Joseph Casasanta and lyrics by Vincent Fagan, and "When the Irish Backs Go

Marching By''—music by Joseph Casasanta and lyrics by Rev. Eugene P. Burke, C.S.C.

46. A new huddle formation, with the quarterback facing the other ten players

47. 9-0-1

48. Don Penza, 1953

49. Don Schaefer

50. Dan Shannon

51. Ralph Guglielmi

52. All-American tackle Frank Varrichione in the 1953 14-14 tie with Iowa

53. Art Hunter and Don Penza

54. Tom Clements

55. Leon Hart, Jim Martin, Mike Swistowicz, Emil Sitko, and Ralph McGehee

56. Bill Wightkin, Ray Espanan and Larry Coutre

57. Once — 1950 (Indiana, Michigan State)

58. Bob Joseph

59. In 1951 when ND beat USC, 19-12

60. On October 5, 1951 — a 40-6 win over Detroit at Briggs Stadium

61. John Lattner, 3 — Heisman, 1953; Maxwell, 1952 and 1953; Ross Browner, 3 — Lombardi, 1976; Outland, 1977; Maxwell, 1977

62. Angelo Bertelli (second in 1941); Joe Theismann (second in 1970); Bill Shakespeare (third in 1935); John Lujack (third in 1946); Nick Eddy (third in 1966); Terry Hanratty (third in 1968); and Ken MacAfee (third in 1977)

63. Joe Heap (1952, 1953 and 1954)

64. Nick Buoniconti

65. Paul Hornung in 1956

66. 1963 — Navy's Roger Staubach was a Heisman Trophy winner.

67. Joe Perkowski, 1961

68. Jim Kelly

69. Ross Browner

70. Angelo Dabiero

71. Bob "Harpo" Gladieux

72. George Connor (1946), Bill Fischer (1948) and Ross Browner (1976)

73. Moose Krause (football and basketball) and Dick Arrington (football and wrestling)

74. There were: 18 Kelly or Kelleys, 16 Murphys, 15 Millers, 15 Smiths, 11 Sullivans, 10 Browns, 9 Williamses and 8 Walshes.

75. Anthony Davis of USC scored 11 against ND.

76. South Bend fans provided a porch-light parade along the bus route to campus where the team was greeted in the fieldhouse by an overflow student crowd.

77. Joe Theismann in 1970

78. Northwestern, which had defeated ND the previous four years

79. Duffy Daugherty

80. Jerome Heavens

81. Parseghian 21 (11 seasons), Leahy 15 (11 seasons), Rockne 10 (13 seasons), Devine 9 (6 seasons), Layden 4 (7 seasons), Brennan 3 (5 seasons), Harper 2 (5 seasons), Anderson 2 (3 seasons) and Kuharich 1 (4 seasons)

82. Joe Restic — 40 punts for 1739 yards

83. Al Hunter (93 yards)

84. Dick Arrington, 1965

85. "Where is *Mark* Clements? I want to shake his hand." — Coach Bear Bryant.

86. Sid Gillman

87. O. J. Simpson

88. Nick Eddy, Jim Lynch, Tom Regner, Alan Page, Pete Duranko, Kevin Hardy, Jim Seymour and Larry Conjar

89. George Goeddeke, Tom Schoen and Paul Seiler

90. Eric Penick

91. Frank Pomarico and Gerry DiNardo

92. Twenty-three games

93. Reggie Barnett

94. Split end Pete Demmerle (he made First Team All-American in 1974)

95. Tim Simon — with minutes to play in a 62–3 victory

96. 1969

97. Mike Kovaleski

98. Missy McCrary, Anne Stringer and Terri Buck

99. Joe Montana

100. Gerry Faust (26)

101. Dave Duerson, 103 returns (1979 to 1982)

102. Tim Brown — 1,157 yards (through 1986)

103. Steve Niehaus

104. The first year of freshman eligibility, 1972

105. Linebacker Bob Crable with 187 tackles (1979)

106. Vagas Ferguson, 1,437 yards (301 carries) in 1979

107. Harry Oliver

108. Tim Koegel

109. Bill Siewe

110. Blair Kiel

111. Tony Hunter

112. John Krimm

FINAL GUN

. . . while her loyal sons are marching onward to victory.

1. Who was the fullback and Walter Camp Second Team All-American who was the important ground-gaining balance to Dorais and Rockne's "air show" in the 1913 Army game?

2. How many passes did Gus Dorais complete against Army in 1913?

3. Who invented the buttonhook pass?

4. Knute Rockne's number-one NCAA career winning percentage record of .881 was immediately preceded by a similarly successful combined effort by eight different head coaches. How similar?

5. What caused the cancellation of the 1910 ND-Michigan game, the beginning of a 33-year cessation?

6. What great All-American halfback preceded George Gipp?

7. What is the number of most consecutive ND wins at home?

8. What was the longest undefeated streak of ND home games?

9. Can you name the ND players who scored those 35 points against West Point that fateful afternoon of November 1, 1913?

10. Who wrote "The Notre Dame Victory March"?

11. What team scored the most points in Irish history?

Notre Dame, Sports Information Department

12. He not only holds the all-time ND rushing record for one season, but he was the first to rush for 1,000 yards in two seasons. Name him.

13. Who played Father Nieuwland in the film *Knute Rockne, All-American*?

14. Who was the pilot of the plane that carried Rockne to his death?

15. What was the flight number of Knute Rockne's ill-fated trip?

16. What type of plane did Rockne board the morning of March 31, 1931?

17. ND defeated heavily favored USC, 27–0, in 1930 due mainly to the effort of a swift substitute halfback disguised as a slower starting fullback. He scored three touchdowns, all on runs of over 50 yards. Name him.

18. Who was the famous politician who was unceremoniously pitched several yards in the air off the ND bench by angry trainer Scrapiron Young?

19. Where is Knute Rockne buried?

20. Which of the Four Horsemen was career total-offense leader of this backfield?

21. Who influenced Jim Crowley of Four Horsemen fame to attend ND?

22. The first ND-USC battle was called by Rockne "the greatest game I ever saw"; the Irish won, 13–12, with two minutes left on a 23-yard touchdown reception by halfback Johnny Niemec.

Name the diminutive lefthanded quarterback who threw the pass.

23. What caused Rockne's phlebitis?

24. Who was the 145-pound "Watch Charm" guard who made Associated Press and United Press First Team All-American on Rockne's last team?

University of Notre Dame, Sports Information Department

25. In addition to Joe Locke, Joe Beach, Austin McNichols, Dean Studer, Ron Bliey, Dave Haley and Mark McLane, this player is the best-known to have worn the number 22.

26. What was Knute Rockne's coaching record against the powerful Army teams of late teens and twenties?

27. How many times did a Rockne-coached team suffer consecutive defeats?

28. Who played opposite Frank Leahy at tackle?

29. Which head football coach served the most university presidents?

30. Who was captain of Rockne's last team?

31. Who is the only coach to have a losing record at ND?

32. What was the "Gridgraphie"?

33. What have been the most penalty yards assessed to an ND team in a game?

34. During the 1935 ND-Ohio State game, Andy Pilney's heroic efforts ended when his knee was mangled after a 36-yard run to the Ohio State 19 yard line with ND behind, 13–12. Who replaced him and threw the winning pass with 40 seconds to go?

35. What was the worst defeat under Elmer Layden?

36. What 1938 Second Team All-American guard and captain later became ND alumni president?

37. This outstanding fullback/captain fumbled only twice in three seasons for the Irish. Name him.

University of Notre Dame, Sports Information Department

38. This late-seventies player went on to pro football prominence as a nose guard for the Cleveland Browns. Who is he?

39. What All-American guard was called the "Baby-Faced Assassin"?

40. ND has had seven players who led the team in receiving yardage three seasons in a row. Name them.

41. Only four receivers in ND history have had 50 or more receptions in a season. Name them.

42. Match these nicknames with the players:
    1. "Peaches"
    2. "Rosy"
    3. "Head"
    4. "Dippy"
    5. "Moose"
    6. "Lank"
    7. "Turk"
    8. "Slip"
    9. "Smousherette"
    10. "Smoush"

43. The 1946 ND-Army game rosters included four players who won Heisman Trophies. Name them.

44. What was the "tackle heard round the world"?

45. This ND quarterback completed passes in 34 consecutive games. Name him.

46. During the Frank Leahy era, only one player led his team in scoring three consecutive years. Who was he?

47. Prior to consensus All-American choice Dave Huffman in 1978, who was the last center to gain such distinction?

48. What was Frank Leahy's last victory as head coach at ND?

49. What ND quarterback won four monograms in a backup role to a starter?

University of Notre Dame, Sports Information Department

50. Name this player who led the Irish in pass receiving in 1984.

51. This former World War II pilot and 1946 All-American centered the 1946 and 1947 national championship teams. Name him.

52. Name the Leahy-era halfback who averaged 17.1 yards in ten carries against Michigan State in 1950.

53. This fleet halfback had an even more sensational day against USC in 1946 when he carried only six

times for 146 yards on 24.4 yards per carry. Name him.

54. Since 1936 the AP has ranked the top twenty college football teams every year except 1962 through 1967, when they ranked only ten. ND has continuously maintained a schedule of top-ranked opponents, and in one year they played seven of ten games against teams ranked in the top 13 in the AP poll. Name that team.

55. Who is the only ND kicker to win an NCAA kick-scoring title?

56. Name the USC halfback who was stopped at the ND one by an inspired Irish defense led by Dick Syzmanski and Jack Whelan to seal a 9–0 1952 victory and deny the Trojans its first undefeated season in 20 years.

57. Frank Leahy returned to football in 1960 to become general manager of what American Football League team?

58. What ND quarterback won most games in Irish career?

59. Name six assistant coaches who served ten years or more at ND.

60. It is well documented that ND has the most Heisman Trophy winners. What school has the second highest number? Name them.

61. Who were the members of the 1963 "Elephant Backfield"?

62. Who was the starting quarterback against Oklahoma in 1957?

63. Who threw the key block allowing Dick Lynch to score the winning touchdown to upset Oklahoma, 7–0, in 1957?

64. What Oklahoma safety was blocked out of the play?

University of Notre Dame, Sports Information Department

65. Only three college players, all Heisman Trophy winners (Glenn Davis, Army; Steve Owens, Oklahoma; and Tony Dorsett, Pitt) have scored more touchdowns in their college careers than this Irish running back. Who is he?

66. Name the placekicker whose 41-yard field goal beat Syracuse, 17–15, in 1962 with no time remaining.

67. When ND broke Oklahoma's famous winning streak in 1957, another Oklahoma streak was broken. What was it?

68. What is the name of the field where that longest consecutive winning streak was broken?

69. In what year did ND hold the dubious distinction of ranking last in the nation in pass defense?

70. Who was the first player to use fifth-year eligibility?

71. How many times has ND won the MacArthur Bowl?

72. What college ranks second to ND in total number of Academic All-Americans?

73. How many of the original sixteen major league baseball parks has ND competed in?

74. What All-American end became an All-Pro and Super Bowl star for the Oakland Raiders?

75. Who holds the ND record for most career touchdown passes thrown?

76. What ND opponent had the best record against Ara Parseghian?

77. Who kicked the winning field goal to beat Alabama, 24–23, in the 1973 Sugar Bowl?

University of Notre Dame, Sports Information Department

78. Name this quarterback who symbolizes in this photograph not only career-ending satisfaction but perhaps the dawn of a bright new era in the second century of ND football.

79. What questionable decision did Coach Bear

Bryant make in the closing minutes of the 1973 Sugar Bowl?

80. Name the Alabama punter who previously had punted 69 yards to the ND one.

81. Who caught a pass by Tom Clements near the end of the 1973 Sugar Bowl "Game of the Century" against Alabama which secured the victory and national championship?

82. Name the co-captains of Ara Parseghian's last ND team.

83. In what season did ND have four different quarterbacks play in the same game?

84. How long was the Texas winning streak that ND broke with the 24–11 win in the 1971 Cotton Bowl game?

85. In the midst of a driving rainstorm in 1971, and losing to Purdue, 7–0, with only 2:28 left in the game, who was the ND defensive end who blocked a Purdue punt for a touchdown (ND won, 8–7)?

86. What season was Ara Parseghian's least productive?

87. In what year did ND first have tri-captains?

88. What great two-time All-American defensive back switched to the offensive unit to catch a 36-yard pass from quarterback Jim Bulger in ND's 1971 Cotton Bowl victory over Texas, 24–11?

89. What years did ND finish out of top ten ranking in the Ara Parseghian era?

90. ND has had only one player at offensive tackle who was both captain and a consensus All-American in the same season. Who was he?

91. What opposing coach tried to use the "power of prayer" to defeat ND?

University of Notre Dame, Sports Information Department

92. This lightly recruited Texan could be ND's seventh Heisman Trophy winner. Who is he?

93. What collegiate football team's shoes were borrowed by ND in the 1973 Sugar Bowl victory over Alabama?

94. Who were the first modern day ND players to play five seasons, all from 1974 to 1978?

95. ND has had 67 consensus All-Americans in its history. Twelve players have achieved this honor in two seasons. Name them.

96. When did the "old-timers" game change to the "Blue and Gold" game?

97. Who is ND's leading career rusher?

98. Which linebacker holds game, season and career record number of tackles?

99. What appellation was bestowed on the football team at the pep rally by basketball coach Digger Phelps prior to the 1977 victory over USC?

100. Who are the co-captains of the 1987 Fighting Irish?

101. Quarterback Terry Andrysiak holds an ND passing record with Angelo Bertelli and Joe Montana. What is it?

102. Name the split end who caught Joe Montana's sideline throw and ran 80 yards to beat North Carolina, 21–14, in 1975.

103. How much time was left in the game?

104. Led by quarterback Joe Montana, ND's 35–34 victory over Houston in the 1979 Cotton Bowl ranks as the greatest comeback in Irish history. With 7:37 left to play, what was the score?

105. With ND still behind, 34–28, Houston's Emmet King was stopped short on fourth and one at its own 29 with 35 seconds to go. Who made this key tackle for the Irish?

106. Who caught Montana's final touchdown throw to tie this game?

107. Who kicked the winning extra point?

108. What makes Joe Montana's comeback heroics during this game more incredible?

109. There were no undefeated teams in the country in ND's 1977 championship season. What team defeated the Irish?

110. When was the first night game at Notre Dame Stadium?

111. In what year did ND first have quad-captains?

112. Through 1986, 2,101 players have played at least one second in at least one varsity game. How many have been mentioned in this book?

University of Notre Dame, Sports Information Department

113. The authors feel that this man will return ND football to the prominence it deserves and will generate an abundance of material for the second edition of *100 Years of Notre Dame Football Trivia*. Who is he?

FINAL GUN — ANSWERS

1. Ray Eichenlaub

2. 14 of 17 for 243 yards

3. Knute Rockne invented it by accident in a game in 1913. While running downfield on a pass, Rockne fell down. When he noticed quarterback Dorais had thrown short, Rockne got up, came back and caught the pass. The play was so successful it was put in the repertoire.

4. Between 1902 and 1917, eight coaches, in the same span of 122 games, achieved a winning percentage record of .840 (slightly less than Leahy at .855 and slightly more than Parseghian at .836).

5.   The University of Michigan claimed that two ND players, Dimmick and Philbrook, were ineligible.

6.   Halfback Stan Cofall (1914–1916); he scored 246 points in 24 games.

7.   Thirty-nine (from November 9, 1907, against Knox, through November 17, 1911, against Michigan State)

8.   Ninety-three – from October 28, 1905, through October 27, 1928. Carnegie Tech ended the streak with a 27–7 victory.

9.   Joe Pliska and Ray Eichenlaub scored two touchdowns, Knute Rockne scored one touchdown, and Gus Dorais kicked the five PATs.

10. Michael Shea, music, and Jack Shea, lyrics

11. The 1912 team scored 389 points in compiling a 7–0–0 record.

12. Vagas Ferguson

13. Albert Basserman

14. Robert Fry of Los Angeles, California

15. Flight 599, Transcontinental-Western, Kansas City to Los Angeles (seven others were killed.)

16. A Fokker Trimotor

17. Paul (Bucky) O'Connor – Rockne had him prac-

tice as the slower Dan Hanley during practice. O'Connor purposely fumbled and stumbled during the week and convinced the Los Angeles sportswriters that the Irish were weak at that position.

18. Major Jimmy Walker of New York (before the Penn game, 1930)

19. Highland Cemetery, South Bend, Indiana

20. Elmer Layden, 3,720 total yards (1,296 yards rushing and 2,424 yards passing)

21. Curley Lambeau

22. Art Parisien (5'7", 148 pounds), a fourth-string quarterback

23. Being hit on the sidelines by three players in the 1929 Indiana game

24. Bert Metzger (1930)

25. Phil Carter, fourth-leading career rusher in ND history

26. 9–2–1

27. Once — 1928 against Carnegie Tech and USC

28. Ted Twomey (1928–1929)

29. Rockne — he served under Rev. John W. Cavanaugh C.S.C., Rev. James Burns C.S.C., Rev.

Thomas Walsh C.S.C. and Rev. Charles O'Donnell C.S.C.

30. Tom Conley (1930)

31. Joe Kuharich (17–23), 1959 to 1962

32. An outdoor electric scoreboard showing the progress of away football games, via Western Union

33. 175 against SMU in 1954

34. Bill "The Bard" Shakespeare

35. When Pitt beat ND, 36–0, in 1936

36. Jim McGoldrick (1936–1938)

37. Milt Piepul (1938–1940)

38. All-American linebacker Bob Golic

39. John Lautar (1934–1936)

40. Don Miller: 1922, 1923, 1924 (31 receptions); John Colrick: 1927, 1928, 1929 (33 receptions); Joe Heap: 1952, 1953, 1954 (69 receptions); Jim Seymour: 1966, 1967, 1968 (138 receptions); Tom Gatewood: 1969, 1970, 1971 (157 receptions); Ken MacAfee: 1975, 1976, 1977 (114 receptions); Tony Hunter: 1980, 1981, 1982 (93 receptions)

41. Jack Snow: 64; Jim Seymour: 53, Tom Gatewood: 77; Ken MacAfee:54

42. 1. Romanus Nadolney (1918)
     2. Jacob Rosenthal (1894, 1895, 1896)
     3. Dick Royer (1956, 1957, 1958)
     4. Fred Evans (1940, 1941, 1942)
     5. Ed Krause (1931, 1932, 1933)
     6. Lancaster Smith (1946, 1947, 1948)
     7. Torgus Oaas (1910, 1911)
     8. Ed Madigan (1916, 1917, 1919)
     9. Bob Donovan (1906)
     10. Dick Donovan (1903, 1904, 1905)

43. Doc Blanchard and Glenn Davis of Army and Johnny Lujack and Leon Hart of ND

44. In the 1952 Oklahoma game, Dan Shannon tackled kickoff receiver Larry Grigg so hard that Grigg did a half-flip in the air and fumbled the ball. The impact was so great that Shannon had to leave the game, through for the day.

45. Ralph Guglielmi (last four games of 1951, all of 1952, 1953 and 1954)

46. Neil Worden — 1951, 1952 and 1953 with 48, 60 and 66 points respectively. (Incidentally, all were touchdowns.)

47. Jerry Groom in 1950

48. December 5, 1953, when ND beat SMU, 40–14

49. Tom Carey: 1951, 1952, 1953 and 1954

50. All-American tight end Mark Bavaro (32 receptions, 395 yards, one touchdown)

51. George Strohmeyer (1946–1947)

52. John Petibon

53. Coy McGee

54. The 1943 national championship team coached by
Frank Leahy played:
    Number-two Iowa Pre-Flight (W 14–13)
    Number-three Michigan (W 35–12)
    Number-four Navy (W 33–6)
    Number-six Great Lakes (L 19–14)
    Number-nine Northwestern (W 25–6)
    Number-eleven Army (W 26–0)
    Number thirteen Georgia Tech (W 55–13)

55. Menil Mavraides with 27 points in 1953

56. Leon Sellers

57. The Los Angeles Chargers

58. Tom Clements

59. Brian Boulac, 13 (1972 to 1982); John Druze, 11
(1941 and 1946 to 1955); George Kelly: 17 (1969 to
1985); Tom Pagna, 11 (1964 to 1974); Joe Yonto, 18
(1964 to 1980 and 1986 to present); and Walter
Ziemba, 11 (1943 to 1953)

60. Ohio State – 5: Les Horvath (1944), Vic Janowicz
(1950), Hopalong Cassady (1955), Archie Griffin
(1974 and 1975)

61. Paul Costa (240 pounds), Jim Snowden (250) and

Pete Duranko (235). Costa and Duranko became defensive linemen, Snowden an offensive lineman. Duranko and Snowden went to the pros.

62. Bob Williams

63. Nick Petrosante

64. Dave Baker

65. Allen Pinkett, 53 touchdowns

66. Joe Perkowski

67. 123 consecutive games without a shutout

68. Owen Field, Norman, Oklahoma (also site of the last ND win before the streak started)

69. 1961: 159.1 yards per game

70. Fullback Gerry Gray in 1962; he had suffered an injury in 1960.

71. Four. 1964, 1966 (tie), 1973 and 1977

72. Nebraska—28 (ND has had 31)

73. Seven: Comiskey Park, Fenway Park, Briggs Stadium, Ebbets Field, Polo Grounds, Yankee Stadium and Municipal Stadium (Cleveland)

74. Dave Casper

75. Joe Theismann, 31 (1968 to 1970)

76. University of Southern California (6–3–2)

77. Bob Thomas (19 yards)

78. Steve Beurlein, a native Californian, after staging the exciting comeback win over USC in the last game of the 1986 season

79. With three minutes to play Alabama punted to ND at the one yard line. The Alabama punter was roughed on the play. Bryant refused the penalty, hoping for an ND turnover.

80. Greg Gantt

81. Robin Weber (he had only one prior pass reception in the season.)

82. 1974: co-captains Tom Clements and Greg Collins

83. 1971 — Pat Steenberge, Bill Etter, Cliff Brown and Jim Bulger

84. Thirty games

85. Fred Swendsen

86. 1972: 8–3–0

87. 1973: Frank Pomarico, offensive captain; Mike Townsend, defensive captain; Dave Casper, team captain

88. Clarence Ellis

89. 1971 (13th) and 1972 (14th)

90. George Kunz (1968)

91. Rice coach Al Conover invited 80 priests as sideline guests in 1973.

92. Tim Brown

93. Tulane's, since ND's new "turf" shoes were ineffective on wet turf

94. Randy Harrison, Pete Johnson and Jeff Weston

95. Frank Carideo (1929–1930), Marchy Schwartz (1930–1931), Bob Dove (1941–1942), George Connor (1946–1947), Johnny Lujack (1946–1947), Bill Fischer (1947–1948), Leon Hart (1948–1949), Emil Sitko (1948–1949), John Lattner (1952–1953), Ross Browner (1976–1977), Ken McAfee (1976–1977) and Bob Crable (1980–1981)

96. The "old-timers" game format of varsity versus former players ended in 1965, when Larry Conjar led the varsity in a 72–0 romp over an old-timers team void of active professional players.

97. Allen Pinkett—4,131 yards, (1982 to 1985)

98. Bob Crable—game: 26 (tied with Bob Golic); season: 187; and career: 521

99. "We are . . . the Green Machine."

100. Chuck Lanza and Byron Spruell

101. Ten straight pass completions over three games in 1985 to tie Bertelli in 1942 against Stanford and Montana in 1978 against Georgia Tech

102. Ted Burgmeier

103. 1:03

104. Houston was leading, 34–12.

105. Freshman defensive end Joe Gramke

106. Kris Haines, with two seconds left

107. Joe Unis

108. He was forced to miss most of the third quarter when his body temperature had dropped to 96 degrees.

109. Mississippi defeated ND, 20–13, in Jackson.

110. September 18, 1982, when ND beat Michigan, 23–17

111. 1985: Tony Furjanic, Mike Larkin, Allen Pinkett and Tim Scannell

112. 422 — including the Kell(e)ys, Murphys, Millers, Smiths, Sullivans, Browns, Williamses and Walshes

113. Lou Holtz